SOVIET WORK ATTITUDES

SOVIET WORK ATTITUDES
THE ISSUE OF PARTICIPATION IN MANAGEMENT

Edited with an introduction by Murray Yanowitch

M. E. SHARPE, INC.
WHITE PLAINS, NEW YORK

MARTIN ROBERTSON
OXFORD

Articles 3, 5, and 6 in this volume are translated by agreement with VAAP,
the Soviet Copyright Agency.

Translated by Michel Vale.

Published simultaneously as Vol. VIII, no. 4 of
International Journal of Sociology

Published in the United Kingdom by
Martin Robertson & Co. Ltd., 108 Cowley Road, Oxford 0X4 1JF

Library of Congress Catalog Card Number: 79-4871
International Standard Book Number: 0-87332-147-2 (U.S. edition)
International Standard Book Number: 0-85520-322-6 (U.K. edition)

Printed in the United States of America

Contents

Introduction

Murray Yanowitch

When a distinct sociological literature began to emerge in
the Soviet Union in the early 1960s, there were good reasons
for some of the Soviet scholars in this area to turn their attention to the study of work attitudes. What could be more appropriate
in a society that proclaimed as one of its goals the transformation of labor into "a prime living need" rather than merely "a
means to subsistence"? And it seemed natural to ask: How much
progress had been made toward developing a distinctive "communist attitude toward work"? What were the behavioral cor-
relates of such an attitude.

Quite apart from the Marxian ideological heritage and its ex-
pectation of changed work attitudes, however, there were more
immediate and "practical" justifications for the serious study
of attitudes toward work. Even a cursory acquaintance with the
Soviet literature on labor problems provides abundant evidence
of chronic difficulties with excessive labor turnover, poor work
discipline, faulty work organization, and disappointing productivity performance. While some of these problems could be
initially regarded as the normal accompaniment of the rapid
and disruptive transformation of a predominantly peasant population into an industrial work force, they did not disappear when
this work force began to be recruited largely from nonpeasant

sources in the 1960s and 1970s. Indeed, in some respects the
problem of mobilizing disciplined and sustained work effort became more serious as educational levels — and along with them,
job expectations — increased and success in meeting production
goals became increasingly dependent on advances in productivity
rather than on large annual increments in the size of the work
force. These were the circumstances in which pragmatic concerns with the sources of work discontent began to replace —
or, at the very least, to supplement — the traditional rhetoric
of "glory to communist labor."

 The selections on work attitudes that appear in this volume
are a small sample of the considerable Soviet literature from
recent years that is directed to studying the experience of work.
The first article, by V. A. Iadov, draws on a pioneering study of
young Leningrad workers' job attitudes in the mid-1960s which
has served as a model for later Soviet efforts in this area.[1]
Perhaps the principal finding of this study, reproduced in Iadov's
article, was that the "richness of content of work," the "creative opportunities" offered by the job, was the single most important factor determining the attitude of the worker toward his
position in the labor process. Without negating the importance
of "material incentives," i.e., wage differentials, Iadov stresses
that if the issue is the relative importance of money wages ver-
sus job content, the answer is unambiguous. Differences in the
degree of work satisfaction experienced by workers in low-
skilled manual jobs and in skilled, "high-content" jobs are substantially greater than differences in the average wage levels
of these groups.

 But the importance of work content as a determinant of work
satisfaction was precisely the problem. Even in the early 1960s,
Iadov claims, the proportion of workers with relatively high educational and cultural levels exceeded the proportion of "high-
content," creative jobs. Moreover, the "disproportion" between
the relatively small number of satisfying jobs and the work aspirations created by rising educational levels could be expected
to increase. In short, the problem of work discontent would become even more serious unless measures were taken to "com-

pensate" workers for the gap between limited work content and
the job aspirations fostered by extended schooling. Iadov's proposals for meeting this problem include job rotation, the provi-
sion of opportunities for "meaningful leisure" (presumably to
offset limited opportunities for "meaningful work"), and the
"development of various forms of participation of workers in
the management of production." Although stated in rather general terms, these proposals illustrate the "practical" orientation of Soviet studies of work attitudes and an explicit recogni-
tion that solutions to the problems of poor work morale require
more than properly designed systems of material incentives.

Like most American studies of work attitudes, Soviet exami-
nations of this area have found that only a minority of workers
voice explicit dissatisfaction with their job situation. But it is
also clear that the frequency of job discontent varies markedly
with workers' age, sex, and education. The evidence offered
in the selection by N. A. Aitov suggests that work dissatisfaction reaches significant proportions among the young, the better
educated, and women. For Aitov the measures required to reduce work dissatisfaction lie in the area of technology design.
Unless technological policy is explicitly adapted to the task of
eliminating the "contradiction" between job content and the educational level of workers, he suggests, a further deterioration
in work attitudes will ensue.

A new direction in Soviet studies of work attitudes emerges
in the last of the three articles on this theme (by V. A. Iadov
and A. A. Kissel'). Contrary to the implicit assumption of
most of these studies, Iadov and Kissel' argue that the level of
job satisfaction is not systematically related to the actual performance of workers in production (their "productivity, conscientiousness, responsibility on the job"). High (or low) levels
of work satisfaction are compatible with both poor and satisfactory work performance. The reason is that "the degree of work
satisfaction provides merely an indication of the degree of a
worker's adaptability to a particular organization and nothing
more," where adaptability signifies the worker's assimilation
of the demands made on him in the work process. Thus the

behind which the plant's Party organization would make its selections? Although the answers to these questions seem all too obvious, we must ask what the proposal to experiment with "elections" of managers signifies. To dismiss the proposal as simply meaningless in the Soviet context would be to miss what the discussion surrounding it reveals.

Kapeliush's report on a "public opinion survey" was only one of several discussions of this issue reported in Soviet publications in the late 1960s.[2] The survey was conducted under the aegis of the Soviet Sociological Association and appears to have been based on a carefully designed poll drawing its respondents from a variety of geographic locales and seven socio-occupational groupings, ranging from ordinary workers to top-level managers. At the very least, the fact that the issue of elections of managers was posed is evidence of a serious concern with providing some semblance — if not the reality — of more participatory forms of economic organization. The very idea of delegating authority from "below," of introducing the accountability of managers to the managed, was certainly a marked departure from the prevailing theory and practice of Soviet management.

Perhaps the most remarkable aspect of Kapeliush's study, as well as of others reported at that time, was not that the issue of elections was raised but that the markedly differing reactions of distinct social groups to the proposal were publicly acknowledged. Kapeliush reports that among ordinary workers and engineers, opponents of the idea of elections did not exceed 5-7 percent; as we move up the managerial ladder from foremen to shop superintendents to plant directors, the proportion opposed to elections increases from one quarter to one third to one half, respectively. To admit that such groups saw themselves as having conflicting interests in the resolution of an issue like the source of managerial authority and accountability was not a common event in Soviet discussions of social and economic issues. The social divisions exposed in the course of this discussion during the late 1960s may help explain why the subject of elections became dormant in the first half of the 1970s. All the more significant, therefore, that it has reemerged more recently. In 1977 the author of the Soviet Sociological Association's 1969 study reviewed his earlier findings, appealed for "an extensive experimental verification of the idea of elections in production," and acknowledged the continuing widespread opposition to the proposal among managers.[3] That the proposal has not been implemented, and is not likely to be in the near future — even in the "safe" form of Soviet-style elections — seems less important than the fact that the proposal has reemerged. The need to create a sense of worker involvement in plant-level decisions has obviously not disappeared.

Other illustrations of the participatory current in Soviet sociological and management literature appear in the articles by Alekseev and Tikhonov. Although couched in the form of studies of work attitudes, both articles are essentially vehicles for posing the issue of worker participation. Alekseev seeks to establish an empirical relationship between the degree of work satisfaction and opportunities for ordinary workers to participate in managerial functions, with the latter implicity defined as decisions bearing on the organization of the production process, the distribution of premiums, and the maintenance of work discipline. Not surprisingly, he finds a positive relationship between satisfaction in work and each of these participatory variables.

Tikhonov points to the limitations of earlier Soviet studies of the labor process, which relied on an excessively narrow approach to the problem of raising the content of work and increasing its "scope for creativity." In earlier studies the stress was typically placed on enriching work by substituting machinery for burdensome manual labor and raising the share of mental or intellectual functions in the total labor process. But the enrichment of work in this view was seen as proceeding exclusively along a horizontal dimension — as a redistribution of functions between man and machine. The vertical component of the labor process, i.e., the distribution of functions between the labor of management and supervision, on the one hand, and the labor of "execution" of work, on the other, was likely to be ignored. The "scope for creativity" in work, however, depends as much on this vertical or social aspect of work-place organization as it does on the relationship between man and machine. More specifically, Tikhonov argues, the enrichment of the work process must be seen as significantly dependent on the "production independence" (or "on-the-job independence") of the worker, the degree to which the functions of planning, organization, and control of the work process are directly delegated to the ordinary worker.

Tikhonov's own findings clearly point to an unduly low managerial component in the worker's overall activity. Fully two thirds of the workers he investigated in the oil industry exhibited "low" to "medium" opportunities for "production independence." Rarely were work tasks planned and distributed by the workers themselves. Not only was the work experience impoverished thereby, but enormous and unnecessarily detailed burdens of administration were imposed on managerial staffs. Some prevailing forms of worker participation in management — and here Tikhonov obviously means fictitious forms like socialist emulation campaigns, attendance at production conferences, "volunteer" (na obshchestvennykh nachalakh) activity to improve productive performance — merely served as "compensation for the social costs of strictly regulated work involving routine execution of directives." Overcoming fragmentation in the work process requires that "the functions of performing work and managing work be combined in the labor process of the direct producer."

In one very important sense these efforts to pose the issue of creating more participatory forms of economic organization in the Soviet Union have failed thus far. None of the findings or proposals included in the studies collected here (or in any other studies that I am aware of) have been translated into institutional changes that would redistribute managerial authority and reduce the enduring barriers between those who plan and control the enterprise's operations and those who execute its work assignments. But these studies do provide a small sample of the available evidence which suggests that pressures for the reform of the work place have not been absent in the Soviet

Murray Yanowitch

Union. Indeed, it is likely that pressures for the democratization of work are a more important feature of Soviet life than pressures for political democratization. The former have a "practical" meaning for Soviet authorities — the possibility of improved work performance — which explains why serious studies of work attitudes and arguments for the democratization of management occasionally receive a hearing. An optimist would hold that these studies and arguments represent only the initial stage of a participatory current in Soviet social and economic thought.

Notes

1. A. G. Zdravomyslov, V. P. Rozhin, and V. A. Iadov, Chelovek i ego rabota, Moscow, 1967. A translation of this volume by Stephen P. Dunn has appeared as Man and His Work, White Plains, International Arts and Science Press, 1970.

2. For other examples see F. M. Rudich, O sochetanii gosudarstvennykh i obshchestvennykh nachal v upravlenii proizvodstvom, Kiev, 1969, p. 76; Ia. E. Stul' and I. O. Tishchenko, "Sociopsychological Principles of Management," in V. G. Afanas'ev, ed., Nauchnoe upravlenie obshchestvom, 1970, no. 4, p. 275.

3. Ia. S. Kapeliush, "In Favor of the Experiment," Literaturnaia gazeta, 1977, no. 35.

SOVIET WORK ATTITUDES

ORIENTATION — CREATIVE WORK

V. A. Iadov

Definitions of man that stressed his difference from other living beings have existed since time immemorial. For example, "man is a thinking animal," or "man is a political animal." As Marx said, you can distinguish man from animals in any way you wish, but he himself begins to differentiate himself from nature through his labor, by virtue of the fact that he adapts the world around him to his needs, transforming it in the process. The development of the productive forces of human society provides the foundations for social progress, for the historical succession of social formations, and for the development of the individual personality. But this process also contains the basic contradiction responsible for the diversity of people's attitudes toward work.

Indeed, the primitive tools of production with which our remote ancestors procured the means for their existence already presupposed some rudimentary division of labor. For example, in a hunting tribe some men performed the role of beaters, while others actually overtook and killed the prey. But all were hunters and freely switched roles; none ever specialized in any one function. The first real division of labor with social

From G. M. Gusev, B. T. Grigorian, I. S. Kon, and L. N. Mitrokhin, eds., Obshchestvo i molodezh', Moscow, 1968, pp. 128-144. Translated by Michel Vale.

underpinnings, namely, the division between male and female labor, has remained with us down to this very day. The further development of the division of social labor led to the formation of classes, some of which possessed the means of production and hence occupied a position of command or authority within the social structure, while others were in the position of slaves, serfs, or proletarians. The progress of mankind has been achieved at the very high cost of the alienation of the individual laborer from the products of his activity, and labor has come to be a forced activity, an externally imposed necessity.

The socialist revolution has abolished the greatest social injustice, namely, the division of society into ruling and exploited classes. But it has not eliminated in one magic stroke the existing division of labor into simple and complex, monotonous and varied, routine and creative, mechanical and organizational, attractive and unattractive. The social division of labor and narrow professionalization are the hallmarks of the world in which we live and in which each of us must find his place.

Scientific socialism differs from magnanimous utopian socialism in that it takes into account the real objective laws and trends of social progress rather than basing itself on good intentions and notions about justice and humanism "in general." "In general" it would be just and humane to maintain an organization of labor in which workers would carry out complex, highly skilled work in alternation with simple work requiring a low level of skill, so that all would be equal in status as working people.

It would also be "just" from the point of view of abstract humanism (and indeed, from the point of view of the narrow conception of equality that identifies it with the leveling out of wages) to limit the opportunities of administrative workers to maintain a large staff responsible for preparing information, seeing to it that decisions are acted upon, and other "bureaucratic red tape."

However, modern production or scientific work is impossible without a clear-cut functional division of labor between differ-

ent kinds of workers and without cooperation designed to achieve
maximum efficiency in the collective process of social production.

Thus, on the one hand, the objective laws of social production
and the development of the material and technical foundations
of communism dictate certain definite requirements with regard to the occupational division of labor, which continues to
grow steadily. (The list of occupations in the population census
for 1926 contained 10,371 designations; in 1939 it contained
19,000; and in 1959 about 30,000.) On the other hand, it is a
commonplace that not all occupations and jobs enjoy a high degree of popularity among the populace or among urban and ru-
ral youth. But the choice of occupation often decides the entire
future destiny and mode of life of a young person. Quite a few
people feel somehow that they are "failures" because they may
be doing some job for which they feel neither attraction nor inclination. This is a problem the sociologist encounters when
he studies the attitudes of youth to work and the tendencies that
appear as constant features of the various types of work motivation and of the general state of satisfaction or dissatisfaction
with one's job.

But what, essentially, have sociological investigations of
young people's attitudes toward work shown? First of all we dis-
cover a number of things which established that public opinion
by no means always judges correctly. The ordinary cast of mind
that guides us in our everyday life does not stand us in very
good stead where the judgments of "common sense" are extended over a broad range of social phenomena in themselves
quite complex, indeed, too complex to be judged on the basis
of individual examples or our own personal experience. Very
often, simple and obvious truths turn out to be much more complex on more careful and deeper analysis and, indeed, are
found not to be truths at all but errors.

One of these errors of "common sense" is the notion that to
be satisfied with one's work is always good and to be dissatisfied is bad. This kind of reasoning is justified if we are considering our own assessment of our own condition. After all,

what can be desirable about a person not being satisfied with
his work? But more careful self-analysis would tell us that
under certain conditions, not being satisfied with a particular
activity may be an incentive for creativity, a quest, or initiative.
Under other conditions, on the other hand, it may impede all
creative activity, frustrate interest in life, lead one to seek
commiseration from others, and become a source of pessimism
and discontent with everyone and everything. In other words,
dissatisfaction is associated with the level of a person's aspirations on the one hand and with the possibilities of realizing
these aspirations in work on the other. The higher the level
of aspirations and demands, the broader the individual's range
of interests, and the richer the content of his needs, the more
likely it will be that such a person will be dissatisfied with
himself and his work. Furthermore, the greater the freedom
of action for fulfilling these demands, the more swiftly will
this state of dissatisfaction find an outlet in a constructive
quest, in creative activity, and in active involvement. If, on
the other hand, high aspirations confront a very narrow range
of real opportunities for their realization, the resulting dissatisfaction has nothing at all constructive about it; indeed, it
thwarts initiative and has the same effect as what we commonly
call "disillusionment with life."

It is not difficult to imagine a quite different relationship between these factors, namely, a situation in which the opportunities for an active, fruitful life and creative work are limited,
and at the same time the individual has only rudimentary interests and modest demands. Such people are completely satisfied with themselves and their work, but this satisfaction has
nothing creative about it; it rather reflects stagnation and com-
placency with what has already been achieved. This is how the
problem of work satisfaction appears from the standpoint of
individual psychology, i.e., from the moral point of view.

A sociological approach to the same set of facts requires
different criteria for assessing and explaining these phenomena. First, it is necessary to ascertain what are the objective
possibilities for applying some creative initiative in one's work

with respect to some particular content of work activity. Furthermore, we must establish how the different groups of occupations with different job contents are distributed within modern industrial production. Third, we must determine the level of demands made by youth on their jobs (or occupations), on what it depends, and what objective factors determine it.

Finally, we must determine trends in the development of the opportunities for realizing particular demands on the one hand and the patterns of change and development in these demands themselves on the other. Only after we have determined all this will we be able to say whether it is "good" or "bad" to be satisfied with one's work, not in the purely individual sense but in the sense in which the terms "good" and "bad" are based on an understanding of real trends in the progressive development of society as a whole. Anything that is in consonance with the progress of society (and its individual members) we will consider "good," and anything that hinders or obstructs that development we will consider "bad" and undesirable. Herein lies the basis of our approach to these phenomena and our efforts to organize labor in such a way as to promote the good with all the means we have at our disposal today.

Our discussion here will be based on data gathered in a sample survey of attitudes toward work among 2,665 workers in Leningrad aged 30 or below, employed in 24 enterprises in various areas of production. (This survey was conducted in 1962-64 by the Laboratory of Sociological Research of Leningrad University. More detailed data are to be found in the book, Chelovek i ego rabota, "Mysl'" Publishers, 1967.)*

Table 1 shows a breakdown of the occupational groups of workers according to the increasing creative potential of the work done in each occupational group: 1. jobs involving unskilled and low-skilled manual labor marked by constant and appreciable physical exertion (a longshoreman, for example);

---

*Editor's note: For an English translation of this volume, see Man and His Work, White Plains, New York, International Arts and Sciences Press, Inc., 1970.

2. work with machinery on a conveyor (a compulsory work pace) requiring occupational training; 3. work on machinery and equipment requiring special occupational training (lathe operator, machine operator); 4. work on semiautomated machines requiring a rather high level of occupational training (automatic equipment operator without the skills required to adjust mechanisms); 5. manual, nonmechanized, highly skilled labor involving the use of special instruments (a fitter-assembler); 6. control and operation of automatic equipment, including skills involved in its adjustment.

Information on the objective results of work (quantity and quality of output, level of initiative of the workers, level of responsibility) was obtained from shop files and from the statements of shop foremen; it was then processed in the form of a qualitative and quantitative assessment. Information on the degree of satisfaction with one's work and area of specialization, and on the level of understanding of the social significance of work, was obtained through survey questionnaires given the same work force. This information was also processed in the form of qualitative and quantitative indices reflecting attitudes toward work and expressed in mutually comparable parameters, with + 1 and − 1 as the highest and lowest ratings, respectively.

As we see from the table, all the parameters characterizing an individual's attitude toward work are closely related to the increasing content of the work itself (showing an increase from left to right) but are not closely related to the average figures for wages. Thus the wage differential between low-skilled manual workers (group 1) and the high-content work of an instrument panel operator (group 6) was only 7 rubles, while the difference in the index of work attitudes was 0.50, or in comparable terms, a 7% increase in wages, given a change in job content, produces an almost threefold increase in the summary index of work attitudes. (The index reflecting quantity, quality, and initiative in work is expressed in relative values with respect to the conditions of work for the particular occupational group.)

Table 1

Indices of Attitudes toward Work among Workers 30 or Less Ranked According to Occupational Group and in Increasing Order of Creative Work Opportunities

Structural indices and characteristics of work attitudes	Occupational groups ranked according to increasing order of creative work opportunities					
	1	2	3	4	5	6
Number investigated	147	307	412	43	285	46
Average wages (rubles)	107.2	87.3	95.1	89.3	97.6	114.2
Level of general education (number of secondary school grades completed)	7.0	8.1	8.3	8.6	8.6	9.4
Index of objective work parameters (output, quality, initiative, responsibility)	−0.17	0.10	−0.03*	0.07	0.11	0.43
Index of the level of work satisfaction	−0.12	0.15	0.18	0.32	0.34	0.22
Index of the level of satisfaction with one's specialty	−0.14	0.15*	0.24	0.27*	0.43	0.35
Index of understanding of the social significance of one's work	−0.31	0.15	0.05*	0.20	0.19	0.26
Summary index of the aforementioned characteristics (weighted average)	−0.185	0.138	0.110*	0.215	0.265	0.315

*Statistically insignificant deviations from the mean according to Student's criterion for a level of significance of 0.05.

It is evident that differences in the content and conditions of
work and in the nature of a worker's needs will have a crucial
influence on the motivational structure of work activity and
hence on the effectiveness of particular work incentives.

According to the data of the same survey, the "hierarchy" of
work motivations ranked in terms of the relative importance
of each motive within the context of their aggregate influence
on the level of general job satisfaction, independent of job content (i.e., the "average" for all 2,665 workers aged 30 or less),
appears as in Table 2.

Table 2

Hierarchy (sequence) of work incentives according to degree of influence on the level of general work satisfaction	Index of signifi- cance of incentives
Work content (to what extent the job requires intellectual effort)	0.72
Wage level	0.61
Opportunities for growth, for improving one's skills	0.58
Diversity in the job (to what extent the job is monotonous or varied)	0.48
State of organization of labor	0.38
Attitude of management toward workers (to what extent manage- ment is attentive to workers' needs and demands)	0.35
Degree of physical stress on the job (does the job cause physical overexertion)	0.32

It is clear that the most important factor determining the
general level of job satisfaction for the young worker is the
content of work, followed then by the wage level and the opportunity for advancement. The last factor is especially important insofar as it encompasses, as it were, the preceding

two most important motivations, i.e., advancement in one's job
means simultaneously an increase in work content and higher
pay. In these cases the material incentive acquires a different
"motivational dressing," i.e., it is regarded by the worker in
terms of the prospects it offers for advancement on the job.
In this form it becomes a most effective factor, especially
among the young generation of the working class. In practical
terms this means that the far-sighted organizer of production
will concentrate his attention on the creation of a well-planned
system of personnel promotion, and in this way he should be
able to tackle successfully the entire nexus of problems associated with improving the stability of the work force in a particular enterprise.

Workers of the older generation show a somewhat different
hierarchy of work motivations. Research findings show that
the motivational importance of sanitary and hygienic working
conditions increases with age, as does the direct motivational
significance of direct payments received by the worker; conversely, prospects for advancement and job content occupy a
somewhat lower place on the motivational scale.

The structure of work motivation is quite different for men
and women. As may be expected from psychophysiological and
social factors reflected in differences in the nature of the demands made by men and women, the latter are extremely sensitive to a whole range of factors bearing on group relationships, particularly the nature of relationships between workers
and the administration. They are more sensitive to sanitary
and hygienic working conditions and prefer mechanized work
even at the expense of job content and the possibility of advancement; they are more inclined to choose work depending on how
far away the job is from home. All these things are completely
understandable and do not require any special clarification.
However, in practice we often apply a policy without regard to
sex and use the same work incentives for both men and women.

We can say that a stable work force and high labor productivity in enterprises with predominantly women employees will,
all other conditions being equal, depend to a considerable de-

gree on the extent to which women's work is mechanized, on satisfactory sanitary and hygienic conditions, on plant amenities (including a system providing for everyday needs on the plant grounds), on how far the enterprise is from the workers' homes, and on how solicitous management is of the workers (and not only with regard to plant matters but in the ordinary human sense of the term as well). In enterprises with a predominantly male work force, of primary importance are the system of advancement and smooth functioning (work pace) of production (stability of pay and not simply its nominal amount), while the level of mechanization of labor, facilities for everyday amenities, and so forth, although retaining some motivational effect, are nonetheless not as important as the factors cited above.

Research findings on the reasons for labor turnover are extremely important in an analysis of the specific features of combinations of work incentives. In contrast to the indices of work attitudes presented above, which refer to a "normal" production situation, a study of the reasons for which workers quit their jobs on their own volition provides us with a picture of the variety of factors that emerge to the forefront in a different, "conflict-type" situation. Wherever we find that job content, pay, and opportunities for advancement do not constitute the core, as it were, of the most important work incentives, and that, on the contrary, other factors supervene, the optimal structure of work incentives is disrupted. Those elements of a work situation that under normal conditions remain at the "periphery" of the motivational structure of labor activity, move into the forefront in a conflict situation and "invade" the very core of the individual worker's motivational structure. They then begin to play a decisive role in determining the nature of the individual's attitude toward work and hence its results.

According to data of a study of the causes of labor turnover at 25 enterprises in Leningrad, covering 10,720 workers who quit their jobs on their own volition, the reasons for quitting (independent of job content and of the individual worker's personal character traits) were as follows (in percentage of the

measurement of work satisfaction as such is less important
than study of the kinds of demands that the economic organization makes on workers and how these demands interact with the
workers' own "dispositional structures" (their orientation toward "creativity and initiative," on the one hand, or toward the
simple "execution of orders," on the other). This approach re-
jects the simplistic identification of work satisfaction as an in-
variably desirable state of affairs so characteristic of earlier
Soviet literature on work attitudes. It implies that the more
interesting question is: If workers exhibit a high degree of work
satisfaction, what is it about their jobs that satisfies them — the
opportunity the jobs provide for "creativity and initiative" or for
the routine "execution of orders"? Hence the relative insignifi-
cance of the level of job satisfaction viewed in isolation from
the whole work environment.

There is obviously a connection between some of the issues
raised in these studies and another theme that has emerged in
Soviet public discourse since the 1960s: the need to extend opportunities for "worker participation in management." We are
not referring here to the constant, ritualistic celebration of of-
ficially designated channels of "participation" (production conferences, the trade union, the enterprise Party organization,
"socialist emulation" campaigns) but to serious efforts to pose
the issue of changing the distribution of managerial authority
and providing opportunities for genuine forms of worker initiative in plant-level decision-making. Some of the principal ways
in which the idea of worker participation — in its real rather
than fictitious sense — has been expressed in recent years appear in the articles by Ia. S. Kapeliush, N. I. Alekseev, and
A. V. Tikhonov.

It may be difficult, at first glance, to take seriously Kapeliush's discussion of the advisability of introducing "elections"
of managerial personnel. Indeed, what meaning could be at-
tached to elections of either lower managerial staffs or plant
directors by a working population long unaccustomed to freely
choosing its leadership at any level of economic or political
organization? Could such elections be anything but a façade

number indicating various reasons):[1]

1. Dissatisfaction with conditions of work activity — 35.6%
   including:
   working conditions — 19.6%
   absence of prospects for growth — 1.8%
   organization of labor — 3.7%
   relationship within the work group and with the administration — 2.5%

2. Dissatisfaction with housing and other everyday facilities —
   27.5%
   including:
   distance of job from home — 8.8%
   no facilities for children (the need to take care of children
   prevents continuation of job) — 9.0%
   change of place of residence — 7.7%
   no hopes of obtaining living space — 2.0%

3. Dissatisfaction with pay — 21.4%
   including:
   size of salary — 21.0%
   no opportunity to switch to an hourly wage — 0.4%

4. Other reasons — 15.5%

   Total   100%

Dissatisfaction with wages was by no means the most important reason for quitting. Material incentives, while retaining
their leading position on the "scale of motives," appeared in
this case in the new "covering" of "working conditions": poor
working conditions that did not allow for stable wages and gave
no prospects of growth were the principal factors responsible
for distorting the optimal structure of work motivation and as
such replaced other motivational factors as the most important, relegating work content and other "basic" elements of
the work situation to marginal roles. Next on the list is a
group of factors which, as we have said, were especially im-

portant to women (for whom everyday amenities have the highest priority), and finally, the actual direct money wages paid to the worker.

An objective analysis of the level of wages at the old and new place of work of persons quitting their jobs confirms the accuracy of our analysis of reasons for quitting. Of the 10,720 workers who quit their jobs, 2,839 took a cut in pay on their new jobs (to obtain an improved job content — a change of occupation or improved organization of labor — more stable pay, and improved everyday amenities); for 4,242 workers the pay remained the same, while 4,545 workers got a higher-paying job. The average wage increase was 2.6 rubles a month for each of these workers but differed markedly depending on occupation. In addition, the higher the wage level on the preceding job, the higher the percentage of persons leaving to take lower-paying jobs, and vice versa.

Thus what general conclusions can be drawn from some of the findings of these sociological and sociopsychological studies?

Obviously there is no such thing as a universal means for providing effective incentives to work, with the exception of one, namely, finding the right combination of all the diverse incentives appropriate to the conditions of production and the composition of an enterprise's work force. This is the first thing.

Second, we can say more or less confidently that among the most important factors influencing decisions with regard to one or another combination of incentives are the following (in order of importance): job content (we found that the lower the the job content, the higher the motivational significance of direct monetary renumeration, while the higher the job content, the more likely the material incentive was to take the form of "possibilities for advancement"): organization of labor; the sex of the particular worker; the level of general education (the lower the level of general education, the higher the motivational significance of direct material incentives; and conversely, the higher the educational level, the more important became the factor of "advancement in work"); age (the younger the worker the greater the motivational importance of possibilities for advancement).

Third, as results of sociological studies have shown, intellectual incentives at work (which we often call moral incentives) generally showed little correlation with the content of work as such but, on the other hand, were highly correlated with the general level of education of the worker, i.e., with the broadness of his outlook, independent of the specific type of work. In other words, the possibilities for effective utilization of moral incentives, namely, a sense of civic responsibility for the results of one's work, a collective interest in the quality of the enterprise's output, socialist competition to achieve better production indices, etc. — the opportunities to activate these incentives for work depend first and foremost on raising the general cultural level of workers and, above all, on the level of their ideological-political awareness as the most important element in the general cultural level of a conscious builder of communism.

Now let us return to the question we posed earlier: is it good or bad to be satisfied with one's work? On what does this depend? What can be done to promote the individual development of each worker, to promote the transformation of labor into a vital inner need of a healthy human being?

From the findings of the sociological studies presented above, it is clear that today's young worker is very sensitive to the functional content of his work: whether it is meaningful, whether it forces him to think and make independent decisions, whether it provides the opportunity for self-improvement, for raising one's skills, for learning something new — all these are the principal factors determining the general state of satisfaction or dissatisfaction with one's work. And this is undoubtedly a progressive phenomenon. It reflects a very high level of intellectual requirements made by workers on their occupations.

We likewise note in the findings of sociologists in the capitalist countries that there, too, there is a discernible tendency

for the functional content of work to exert a strong influence
on the general state of work satisfaction. Unfortunately, the
Western sociologists who undertake such analyses do not always take into account one very important factor, namely, the
situation on the labor market (the fluctuations in employment
in a given area or a given branch of industry). But the insta-
bility of a capitalist economy has a direct impact on the relative importance of the functional content of work among all the
various factors determining general work satisfaction. Let us
illustrate this on the basis of one example.

In 1949 two studies were made of workers in the textile industry
in the United States. One of them was in an area of relatively full
employment (a study by L. Reynolds and J. Shuster). The other was
conducted in an area where unemployment was a full 15% higher
than its normal level (which the authors did not indicate; the study
was done by C. Meyers and G. Shultz). The methods used in both
studies were comparable. Let us take a look at the findings:

Table 3

Reasons for job satisfaction	Distribution of responses (in percentage of total)	
	in area with high unemployment	in area with low unemployment
Economic reasons: job security, pay, possibilities of advancement on the job	53	22
Reasons associated with the nature of the job itself, the content and conditions of work	21	38
Reasons associated with relationships between workers and management	8	37
Other reasons	1	13
Total number surveyed	150	150

The findings indicate that in a period of unemployment, incentives having to do with the content of work decline sharply in importance for the worker; they are replaced by other economic interests, interests associated primarily with job security (regardless of work content). But during a period of relative stability in the labor market, incentives having to do with work content compete with other motivations, such as relationships between management and labor, i.e., between representatives of the interests of the two classes, worker and employer.

If we compare these findings with those obtained in studies by Soviet sociologists, it becomes quite clear that the paramount position of motives having to do with the content of work among young Soviet workers is by no means a chance occurrence but is due to those social changes that have taken place in the course of socialist reconstruction of our society.

It is also important to note that the tendency for incentives associated with the content of work to move into the forefront among the entire variety of work incentives should increase as the general educational level of workers increases, as their general cultural outlook expands, and as their need for creative work grows. This is also one of the progressive trends of our times.

However, we must not ignore the fact that changes in work content are taking place at a slower rate than the increase in the educational level of workers. According to our calculations, the percentage of workers employed in occupations offering relatively great creative opportunities, fully adequate to the needs of people with an education of more than seven years of secondary school, was approximately 30.8% in Soviet industry in 1962. The proportion of persons employed in occupations with relatively low creative opportunities, adequate to the demands of workers with a seven-year education and below, was 69.1%. According to the statistics of the Central Statistical Administration of the USSR, in 1962 the proportion of workers with a seventh-grade education or less was 38.6% (compare this with the proportion of workers employed in relatively creative types of labor — 30.8%). In other words, even in 1962 there was a "surplus" of workers with a relatively high level

of education who were unable to satisfy their needs for relatively high-content work activity. Moreover, according to data
of the Central Statistical Administration, the rate of increase
in the number of skilled and highly skilled workers lags somewhat behind the rate of increase in the number of workers with
more than seven years of education: in the nine-year period
from 1955 through 1963, the share of the former increased by
2.1%, while the share of the latter increased by 3.4%.

As the gap between the level of skills and the level of general education of workers decreases, the disproportion between
the opportunities for creative work and the level of demands
of the highly educated younger generation entering the work
force increases. What is more, this disproportion tends to increase as a result of the sharp rise in the number of secondary
school graduates entering industry and the lowering of the average age of the working class (the so-called "demographic
echo" of the war), on the one hand, and of the comparative stabilization of the ratio between the number of persons employed
in occupations of a relatively creative and relatively noncreative nature, on the other. This stabilization is rooted in the
particular features of the present stage of technical progress
in our country, namely, the stage of complex mechanization
of production. According to the calculations of the Soviet econ-
omist A. Veinberg, the decrease in the relative share of workers performing simple, unskilled work (owing to the mechanization of packing and warehouse work and similar jobs) has been
accompanied by a decrease in the relative importance of complex manual labor of the manufacturing or craft type (machin-
ists-tool makers, gauge makers, etc.). The relative share of
workers occupied in jobs offering moderate creative opportunities (constant occupations, i.e., machine operators) is increasing, while the relative share of automatic machinery supervisors is growing at an extremely slow pace.

However, in the next stage of the technological reequipping
of industry, namely, the comprehensive automation of production, the relative importance of comparatively creative and
noncreative jobs will change markedly. A decisive shift will

take place in the content of the mass of occupations in production. According to calculations of economists, the ratio of
maintenance workers to operators under conditions of large-
scale serial production in work on nonautomated equipment is
1 : 12 or 1 : 15, while in work on automated assembly lines it is
1.6 : 1. This means that the comprehensive automation of production will be accompanied by a ratio of highly creative occupations to occupations of a relatively monotonous work content of about 1.6 : 1, or more. Such are the prospects for the
future.

Thus the majority of today's working youth are looking for
ways to apply their efforts in which they will be able to improve
their competence, to grow on the job, so to speak; they are looking for work with a relatively creative content. But for the
present such possibilities are by no means available every-
where. They are particularly limited in those branches of industry employing assembly-line production in which operations
are highly differentiated. However, there are some real means
available to "amortize" the disproportion cited above between
the growing needs for work of high content and the possibilities
that modern production offers to meet these needs.

One such possibility is switching jobs [peremena truda],
movement of the work force, in particular, advancing to jobs of
higher creative content. Statistics show that the average dura-
tion of work in an occupation is lowest in those occupations offering little creative opportunities and in which the skill "ceil-
ing" is reached quickly. This is the case, for example, with
assembly-line operators in the light-bulb industry (where average job stability is about three years) and in a number of
other occupations. In these jobs there is a much more rapid
turnover of personnel as compared with other occupations
where the content and prospects of jobs are richer. Life itself
"regulates," as it were the movement of the work force, so
that it reflects patterns that promote the development of the
individual worker. And Soviet sociologists and economists are
quite right when they point out that this work force turnover
has not only negative features but positive aspects as well. It

reflects in broad outline the economic and social law of job switching, which our society should master more fully than it does today. Just as society plans production that temporarily operates at a loss (for example, new sectors of industry), so it can also plan for certain losses from the inevitable "turnover" of the work force in the least popular jobs as a result of the increased social "profits" obtained by society from the improved moral and psychological attitudes of workers who can look forward to prospects for growth, constant improvement, and intellectual and material advancement from their occupational endeavors.

Another important factor serving to "amortize" this contradiction is the development of various forms of participation by workers in the management of production. The highly educated worker found today in our factories is capable of assuming greater responsibility in matters relating to production and the organization of labor. Clearly, to develop all forms of initiative in the area of mangement, especially under conditions of our new system of economic incentives for labor in production, much more must be done than has been done up to now. There is considerable scope here for work by scientists, by leaders of industry, and by social organizations in production.

The third possible channel is the systematic and steady improvement of the various forms of meaningful leisure time. Leisure time and its content are closely bound up with occupational activity. According to the observations of Western sociologists, under conditions of capitalist production monotonous and uniform work makes the time spent after work just as meaningless. A dynamic personality stereotype is created, a unique form of inertia that sets in during production and continues to operate beyond it.

According to data of soviet researchers who have investigated workers' time budgets, signs of such a tendency are also evident in our country. However, in a socialist society there are effective ways to counteract these inertial forces. For example, the education and upbringing of the rising generation has different goals and objectives, and the content of all our

public information and education is designed to meet the growing needs of the individual worker. These possibilities are
also associated with the objectives of all our social organizations, e.g., the party, the Komsomol, and the trade unions.
Their aim is not to standardize and eradicate differences in
tastes, habits, hobbies, etc., but on the contrary, to contribute
to and promote the comprehensive development of every individual and to create social conditions under which a diversity
of interests can find a diversity of means, methods, and channels for their satisfaction. Unfortunately, however, although
we have a clear understanding of this aim, we have given too
little thought to the concrete ways, modes, methods, and re-
sources for achieving it. Aside from the special studies and
research in this area that still remain to be done by Soviet sociologists, a great deal can be contributed by Komsomol organizations and volunteer groups of enthusiasts. Anything that
they might do to promote "rationalization" in this area is no
less important than what they can do to rationalize production.

We have acquired the habit of looking for a quick solution
to all social problems on the order of the day; not finding such
a quick and satisfactory solution, we criticize those whose
"duty" it is to forsee and predict everything. That is the psychology of many young people, and not only the young. It has
its roots in the relatively recent past, when the initiative and
sense of responsibility of each citizen was suppressed and not
given room to develop freely and fully. Today, through the efforts of the Communist Party we have created much more favorable conditions for the development of creative initiative
and for increasing the civic responsibility of every Soviet citizen. One of the most important tasks in the education of the
young citizen of our country is to create the kind of environment for his everyday activities (in school, in production, in
everyday life) in which the young person will be able to really
feel his responsibility to society and to the collective. The
limits of creativity are by no means exhausted by one's activity on the job or by amateur pastimes. The most valuable aspect of the development of the human personality in the com-

munist era, which began in October 1917, is the sense of civic responsibility for society, for one's country, and for one's collective. This priceless character trait of the Soviet man can and must be fostered by the Leninist Komsomol.

Note

1. See L. S. Bliakhman, A. G. Zdravomyslov, and O. I. Shkaratan, Dvizhenie rabochei sily na promyshlennykh predpriiatiiakh, Moscow, "Ekonomika" Publishers, 1965, pp. 53-54.
The data shown here are very similar to those obtained in other studies in Novosibirsk, Moscow, and Sverdlovsk (see the results of surveys in several cities and districts, ibid., pp. 56-57).

2 THE INFLUENCE OF JOB CONTENT ON WORK ATTITUDES

N. A. Aitov

Job content, i.e., the set of functions performed by a worker in production, cannot help but affect his attitude toward work. Work attitudes are an important factor that influences not only labor turnover but also other forms of movement of the work force (job changes as a result of technological progress, social mobility). In very many cases a worker's decision to shift to a new job or to move into a different social group is based on the same set of reasons as his decision simply to leave an enterprise, which we classify as labor turnover.

We shall be examining the problem of work content from the point of view of repetitiveness and monotony of work and the productive functions performed by workers.

Of course, we must immediately distinguish the main work force (machine operators) from others. In the population we studied, machine operators constituted 65.6% of the total. To these must be added 15.9% of workers engaged in technical

From N. A. Aitov, Tekhnicheskii progress i dvizhenie rabochikh kadrov, Moscow, "Ekonomika" Publishers, 1972, pp. 72-90. The material discussed here is based on questionnaires administered to 15,000 workers in the machine-building industry in the period October 1967 to January 1968. Translated by Michel Vale.

servicing of machines (adjusters, fitters, etc.). Consequently,
about 81.5% of all our workers were engaged directly in the
production of output. Auxiliary workers (loaders, carriers,
storeroom workers, etc.) constituted 8.3%, junior service personnel 1.3%, and other workers (mainly construction workers,
repair men, transport workers, and communications workers)
were 8.9%.

Machine operators and adjusters are the most skilled groups
in the working class. At the highest level of skill were adjusters
(with a wage grade of 3.7), followed by machine operators engaged in fulfilling individual orders (grade 3.3), other workers
(grade 3), machine operators engaged in large-scale serial
production (grade 2.8), auxiliary workers (grade 2.7), and
other machine operators (grade 2.6). The average wage grade
for all machine operators was 2.8. The highest paid were machine operators engaged in fulfilling individual orders, followed
by adjusters, with machine operators engaged in large-scale
serial production in third place, machine operators engaged
in small-scale serial production in fourth place, workers in
other kinds of work in fifth place, auxiliary workers in sixth
place, and junior service personnel in seventh place. It must
be borne in mind that the study was carried out before the
January 1, 1968, wage increase for machine operators.

The influence of monotony or diversity in a job already
showed up in the workers' answers to the question whether they
liked their work. Negative answers to this question were given
by 7.1% of the machine operators engaged in large-scale serial
production, 7% of those engaged in small-scale serial production, 5.8% of those engaged in fulfilling individual orders, and
only 3.9% of the adjusters. On the other hand, 19.3% of the
junior service personnel, 13.2% of auxiliary workers, and 4.6%
of the workers engaged in other kinds of work answered no to
this question. Characteristically, the differences among the
three groups of machine operators with regard to what they did
not like about their jobs were appreciable only on certain points
(see Table 1).

All these factors also influence labor turnover. A total of

Table 1

Distribution of Machine Operators and Factors
They Did Not Like in their Work (in % of
reason cited by each group)

	Monotony in work	Did not like anything	Did not like job itself
Machine operators in large-scale serial production	5.2	3.5	1.5
Machine operators in small-scale serial production	4.8	2.8	2.0
Machine operators fulfilling individual orders	1.8	2.6	1.7

21.3% of the machine operators engaged in large-scale serial production, 21.3% of those engaged in small-scale serial production, and only 16.8% of those engaged in fulfilling individual orders said they wanted to leave their places of work.

The effect of monotony and diversity in a job on work attitudes shows up clearly in the distribution of workers in accordance with their answer to the question about the degree of monotony in their work. Those who wanted to leave their work places represented 21.6% of those who produced the same piece all the time or performed the same operation, 21.5% of those who performed only one operation for a whole month, 18.5% of those who performed one operation on one day and another operation on the next, and 16.8% of those who performed several different operations on the same day. [1] The coefficient of correlations among these factors was 0.52.

Whereas 15.1% of those who performed the same operation the whole time said that they wanted to leave their work be-

cause they wanted to change their occupations and because they
did not like their jobs, 8.7% of those who performed several operations during a day invoked these reasons, i.e., almost half
as many.

Young and highly educated workers were the most discon-
tented with the monotony in their work. Those who answered
that they did not like their job because of its monotony included
1.1% of workers with fourth- to sixth-grade education, 4.1% of
workers with eighth-grade education, 5.9% of workers with
ninth-grade education, 7.3% of workers with tenth-grade education, 10% of workers with incomplete higher education, and 33%
of workers with higher education. No worker with only first-
through third-grade education gave this reason.

The average length of time in their field of specialization
was 5.8 years for those who said that they did not like their
work because of its monotony, while the figure was 9 to 15
years for persons who pointed to other factors. Among young
workers women reacted most sharply to work monotony, while
it was men who did so among older workers.

A second important factor in work content is the functions
carried out by the worker in production. Ia. B. Kvasha drew
up a classification of the instruments and tools of labor in accordance with their degree of automation; Z. I. Fainburg and
G. P. Kozlova introduced some refinements into this classification by distinguishing the following subgroups of the tools
and instruments of labor with regard to the degree of their
technological sophistication and the degree of automation: [2]

1. Manual instruments and the simplest contrivances.
2. Mechanized and electric instruments.
3. Machines without a fixed connection between the functioning component and the object of labor, i.e., machines functioning only when operated with their service personnel.
4. Solitary semiautomatic machine.
5. Solitary automatic machinery.
6. Semiautomatic units, assemblies and combines.
7. Cyclical units (assemblies, combines).
8. Automatic units, self-adjusting systems with automatic

maintenance of preassigned schedule, automatic adjustment.

We used the Fainburg and Kozlova classification as our basis for classifying different kinds of machinery and equipment. But we had to simplify this classification because we found that there were so few workers involved in the different kinds of automation that when we broke them down into several groups, the law of large numbers would no longer have been in force, and random factors would have come to dominate. Hence we adopted the following classification:

1. Manual instruments and the simplest contrivances.
2. Mechanized and electric instruments.
3. Machinery without a fixed connection between the functioning component and the object of labor.
4. Semiautomatic machinery (solitary).
5. Machinery with programmed control.
6. Automatic and cyclical units, single automatic machines.

Of course, this classification by no means includes all tools; it is a classification only of those tools used by the workers covered in the present study.

We found that workers rated their work on these tools differently. The figures for workers who did not like their jobs were as follows:

1. 31.8% of workers using manual instruments and the simplest contrivances.
2. 37.8% of those using mechanized and electric instruments.
3. 35.3% of those using machinery without a fixed connection between the functioning component and the object of labor.
4. 37.5% of those using semiautomatic machinery.
5. 3% of those using machinery with programmed control.
6. 25% of those using automatic and cyclical units and single automatic machinery.

Workers using machinery with programmed control were the most satisfied with their jobs. They were followed in descending order by workers on automatic machinery; workers using manual instruments; workers using machinery without

fixed connection between the functioning component and the object of labor; workers using mechanized or electrical instruments; and in last place in popularity, work on semiautomatic
machinery.

However, the different groups of workers had different attitudes toward the same kinds of work. To study the influence
of technical equipment on the work attitudes of the different
groups of workers, we subdivided our sample population into
eighteen standard groups differing in sex, age, and education.
Three age groups were distinguished: young workers (under
30), middle-aged workers (30 to 45), and older workers (over
45). This breakdown was based on psychological differences
among these age groups and differences in their attitudes toward the conditions, organization, and content of work.

We distinguished three groups with regard to education: the
first — workers with a low level of education (first to seventh
grades); the second — workers with eighth- to ninth-grade education. These were chiefly young workers who were attending
evening schools. Most had left daytime schools for work because of lack of desire to study, discipline problems, or for
economic considerations. Finally, there was a third group —
workers with secondary or more than secondary education.
This groups had particularly high demands on the content of
work.

Let us subdivide our population into eighteen standard groups
and examine the attitudes of workers in these groups toward
work on different instruments and tools.

The first group comprised men under 30 with first- to seventh-grade education (5.6% of the workers). A total of 35.7%
of them did not like their work. This group was in fifth place
with regard to the degree of dissatisfaction with the particular
kind of work they did. The most satisfied within this group
were workers on semiautomatic machinery (all workers operating these machines were satisfied with their work); in second
place were workers doing work on automatic units and machinery (75% were satisfied); in third place were workers using
mechanized or electrical instruments (67.9% were satisfied);

in fourth place were workers on machinery without fixed connections between the operating unit and the object of labor
(58.1% were satisfied); in fifth place were workers with manual
instruments and the simplest devices (25% were satisfied); while
in last place were workers on machines with programmed control (100% were dissatisfied).

The first group included a category of people rarely encountered today: young workers with extremely low education,
mainly migrants from the countryside. The urban members'
of this group had been for the most part "problem children"
in the past, and in school they were the laziest, most incapable,
did not want to learn, and lacked discipline. Findings from
studies of time budgets and value orientations carried out by
R. A. Zlotnikov in Bashkiria have shown that this group of
workers has a very low level of value orientation: in their free
time from work they do not read books, do not go to the theater
or movies, and have very limited intellectual needs. This cultural value orientation is also linked to a very specific orientation with regard to work: they liked work that was physically
easy and intellectually simple. They preferred semiautomatic
machinery to machinery with programmed control, which required thought and study.

The second group included women under 30 with first-
through seventh-grade education (3.8% of the workers). This
group was in first place among all groups with regard to the
degree of dissatisfaction with their work: 66.7% of all those
questioned did not like their jobs. The most attractive kind
of work for this group was work on automatic assembly lines
or machinery (100% satisfied), although, to be sure, this kind
of work was done by only 10% of the group members. In second place was work with manual instruments and simple contrivances; in third place — work with machinery without fixed
connection between the operating unit and the object of labor
(61% satisfied); in fourth place — work with mechanized or
electric instruments (56.5% satisfied). The largest portion
of this group were junior service personnel and auxiliary
workers who, on the whole, were no more satisfied with their

work than machine operators.

The interests of this group of girls and young women were not very much oriented toward productive labor, since women with low education do not have very great prospects of moving up the ladder within the job hierarchy. The principal problems bothering them were starting a family and everday family problems. Their pay was low, and their work was not very interesting.

The third group (men under 30 with eighth- to ninth-grade education; 7.5% of the workers) was in third place with regard to dissatisfaction with their work (40%). The most attractive kind of work for this group was work on machinery with programmed control, followed in second place by work with manual instruments, in third place by work with automatic machinery, in fourth place by work on semiautomatic machinery, in fifth place by work with mechanized or electrical instruments and in sixth place by work on machinery without fixed connections between the operating unit and the object of labor. A total of 18.5% of this group were attending evening and technical schools. These people made high intellectual demands on their work, and it was precisely this segment of the group that liked work on machinery with programmed control or on automatic units and machinery. Another segment of this group was exstudents who had not done very well in school and were employed in comparatively uncomplicated work. Their interests had not yet crystallized; they were still trying to "find themselves," as well as a good job. For the time being many of them were satisfied with simple manual work.

The fourth group (women under 30 with eighth- and ninth-grade education; 4.7% of the workers) was in twelfth place with regard to dissatisfaction with their jobs (21% of those questioned in this group were not satisfied).

This group was most satisfied with work on semiautomatic machinery, followed by work with manual instruments and simple devices, with work on automatic machinery in third place, work on machinery without fixed connections between the functioning unit and the object of labor in fourth place, work with mechanized electrical instruments in fifth place (a total of 63% of all the workers of this group did this kind of work).

Only 5.6% of this group were attending school; their value orientation was chiefly centered on establishing their family and resolving everyday problems. Work on semiautomatic machinery not requiring any intellectual stress was the most attractive for the majority of this group.

The fifth group (men under 30 with tenth-grade education or more; 10.3% of the workers) was in tenth place with regard to dissatisfaction with their work (28% were not satisfied). In first place with regard to attractiveness of the work were jobs on automatic machinery; in second place — jobs on machinery with programmed control; in third place — work on mechanized instruments; in fourth place — work with machinery without a fixed connection between the functioning unit and the object of labor; in fifth place — work on semiautomatic machinery; in sixth place — the work of junior service personnel and auxiliary personnel.

The value orientation of this group in the sphere of work was determined by their high level of education: they had a clearly pronounced inclination for complex and interesting work and were dissatisfied with simple, especially monotonous, work. Although the degree of satisfaction with work was comparatively high for this group of workers, the turnover and movement of the work force in this group was on the whole much higher than in the others. First, dissatisfaction with simple work was most acute in this group, since the contradiction between the rise of education and technology shows up most sharply here. Second, a considerable number of these workers were attending higher educational institutions in the evening or taking correspondence courses, i.e., they were preparing to enter the social group of the intelligentsia.

The sixth group (women under 30 with secondary education or higher; 11.7% of the workers) occupied ninth place with regard to dissatisfaction with their work (29.7% of these workers did not like their jobs). The distribution with regard to the attractiveness of jobs was exactly the same as in the fifth group.

The seventh group (men 30 to 45 with first- through seventh-grade education; 17.6% of the workers) was in seventh place with regard to dissatisfaction with their jobs. As regards attractiveness of their work, the order of preference was as follows: work on semiautomatic machinery; work on machinery with programmed control; work on machinery without fixed connection between the functioning unit and the object of labor; work on automatic machinery; work on mechanized and electrical instruments; work with manual instruments and simple devices.

This group included experienced and skilled workers (who liked work on machinery with programmed control and on automatic machinery), but not very literate and semiskilled workers predominated; they were completely satisfied (as were all workers with seventh-grade education or less) with work on semiautomatic or mechanized instruments.

The eighth group (women 30 to 45 with first- through seventh-grade education; 15.6% of the workers) was in seventeenth place with regard to job dissatisfaction. Most of them liked work with manual instruments or simple devices, or, next, work on automatic machinery, with work on machinery without fixed connection between the functioning unit and the object of labor in third place, work with mechanized instruments in fourth place, and work with semiautomatic machinery in fifth place.

The workers of this group (80-90%) liked all kinds of work they did; an exception was work on semiautomatic machinery, which half of the workers did not like. The women in this group had attained a certain position in life that on the whole satisfied them; they were not thinking of changing their jobs. They had neither the desire nor the opportunity to do so (low education, family concerns). On the other hand, dissatisfaction with housing and everyday facilities was the greatest for them.

The ninth group (men 30 to 45 with eighth- to ninth-grade education; 3.8% of the workers) was in sixteenth place with regard to job dissatisfaction (14.2% were not satisfied with their

jobs). Work on machinery with programmed control was a fa-
vorite for them, followed in descending order by: work on machinery without fixed connection between the operating unit
and the object of labor; work on automatic machinery; work
on mechanized or electric instruments; work with manual instruments or simple devices; work on semiautomatic machinery.

The value orientation with respect to work was directed toward complex work. This group consisted chiefly of experienced skilled personnel with a relatively high level of education.

The tenth group (women 30 to 45 with eighth- and ninth-grade
education; 3.4% of the workers) was in thirteenth place with
respect to the number of those who answered that they did not
like their jobs (21%). They liked the following types of work
in descending order: work on semiautomatic machinery; work
with manual instruments; work with automatic units or machinery; work with mechanized or electric instruments; work
on machinery without fixed connection between the operating
unit and the object of labor. They preferred simple labor.
Their demands on their jobs and on job content were slightly
greater than women of the same age with less education (the
eighth group). Evidently, a small difference in education in
this age group does not cause any difference in value orientation with respect to labor. The educational factor generally
has more of an impact among young people.

The eleventh group (men 30 to 45 with tenth-grade or higher
education; 3.2% of the workers) occupied eleventh place with
regard to the number of persons who said they did not like their
jobs (21.5%). Work on semiautomatic machinery was the most
popular, followed in descending order by: work on machinery
with programmed control; work with manual instruments or
simple devices; work on mechanized or electrical instruments;
work on automatic machinery; work on machinery without fixed
connection between the operating unit and the object of labor.
The age factor, and not education, also influenced the choice
of jobs.

The twelfth group (women 30 to 45 with a tenth-grade educa-

tion or higher; 1.9% of the workers) occupied eighth place with
regard to the number of persons who said they did not like their
jobs (31.6%). The kind of work they preferred over all others
was work with manual instruments and simple devices. This
was followed in descending order of preference by: work on
semiautomatic machinery; work with mechanized or electrical
instruments; work on machinery without fixed connection between the operating unit and the object of labor. The members
of this group did not do the other kinds of work. For the women
of this group, education played almost no role in shaping a value
orientation toward work.

The thirteenth group (men over 45 with first- to seventh-
grade education; 6.1% of the workers) occupied seventh place
with regard to the number of those who answered that they did
not like their jobs (33.3%). Most popular in this group was
work with manual instruments or simple devices, followed in
descending order by: work on machines without fixed connection between the operating unit and the object of labor; work
with mechanized or electrical instruments; work with automatic machinery. The value orientation of this group was determined by age and education: they liked relatively simple
but skilled work that required little education but long training
and habituation to perform.

The fourteenth group (women over 45 with first- to seventh-
grade education; 3.4% of the workers) was in fifteenth place
with regard to the number of negative answers to the question
whether they liked their jobs (15.8%). This group preferred
work with manual instruments or simple devices, followed in
second place by work on automatic machinery, in third place
by work on machinery without fixed connection between the
operating unit and the object of labor, and in fourth place by
work on semiautomatic machinery. This group did not do any
of the other kinds of work. The value orientation of this group
was in general the same as in the preceding group.

The fifteenth group (men over 45 with eighth- to ninth-grade
education; 0.6% of the workers) was in last place with regard
to the number who said that they did not like their job, i.e.,

none of them said that they did not like their jobs. They worked
on machinery without fixed connection between the operating
unit and the object of labor and also with mechanized and electrical instruments. These workers were usually in the highest
wage categories. We found in general that the higher the wage
category, the less the dissatisfaction with work.

The sixteenth group (women over 45 with eighth- to ninth-
grade education; 0.2% of the workers) was in fourth place with
regard to the number of those not satisfied with their jobs
(37.5%). Without exception, all of those employed on machinery
without fixed connection between the operating unit and the object of labor liked their jobs. This was followed in descending
order by: work with manual instruments or simple devices;
work using mechanized or electrical devices (none of those
doing this kind of work liked their jobs). The value orientation
with regard to work was typical of that for experienced, skilled
workers with long years of work experience behind them.

The seventeenth group (men over 45 with tenth-grade education and higher; 0.4% of the workers) was in fourteenth place
with regard to the number of those who did not like their jobs
(16.6%). This group liked work with mechanized instruments
best, followed by work on machinery without fixed connection
between the operating unit and the object of labor, and in last
place, work with manual instruments or simple devices (only
50% liked it). By the age of 45 these workers had already for-
gotten the theoretical knowledge they had learned in secondary
school. Hence the members of this group did not aspire to
master new complicated technology (automatic units, modern
machinery with programmed control) and were oriented toward customary old technology, which they knew quite well
and which paid well.

The eighteenth group (women over 45 with secondary education; 0.2% of the workers) were in second place with regard
to the number of those who did not like their jobs (50%). This
is explained by the fact that at this age women are relatively
less interested in their work and are more concerned with
domestic matters. Furthermore, almost all of them had jobs

using manual tools or simple devices, which could not satisfy
them.

These, then, were the attitudes of the different groups of
workers toward their jobs. Our findings do not tell us whether
the members of any group value or do not value a particular
kind of work (our survey was not conducted to rate the different kinds of work). Rather, they show whether the people performing specific kinds of jobs liked them. If members of a
particular group were not involved in jobs on machinery with
programmed control, they were not asked whether they liked
work on this kind of machinery.

On the whole, 29.9% of workers under 30 did not like their
work, with the corresponding figures being 22.2% for those between 30 and 45, and 23.3% for those over 45.

What were the main trends in attitudes toward different kinds
of work in the light of data drawn from an analysis of the different groups?

1. Work with manual instruments or simple devices. Women
were more interested in this kind of work than men. This interest increases with age and decreases sharply with an increase in educational level.

2. Work using mechanized or electrical instruments was
preferred more by men, mainly oder men. Education had no
appreciable influence on attitude toward this kind of work.

3. Women liked work on machines without fixed connection
between the operating unit and the object of labor somewhat
more than did men; the number of positive answers to the question whether they liked this kind of work increased with age.
Educational level had little influence on attitude toward this
kind of work.

4. Work on semiautomatic machinery. In groups with a low
level of education, men liked this kind of work better than
women; while in groups with a relatively high level of education, women preferred it. Older workers with a low level of
education like this kind of work most of all; young educated
workers had a negative attitude toward it.

5. Work on an automatic unit or automatic machine. Persons with eighth- to ninth-grade education and of middle age liked this kind of work best; attitude toward this kind of work worsened with age.

6. Work on machinery with programmed control. Attitude toward this kind of work improved with increasing educational level and age.

Thus the ranking of jobs according to workers' preferences was as follows:

1. Work on machinery with programmed control.
2. Work on automatic units or machines.
3. Work with manual instruments or simple devices.
4. Work on machinery without fixed connection between the operating unit and the object of labor.
5. Work using mechanized or electrical instruments.
6. Work on semiautomatic machinery.

What was it that people did not like about working with different kinds of instruments of labor?

The number of complaints of job monotony decreased with the increasing complexity of technology; on the other hand, complaints about frequent changes of operations increased. Workers using more complicated technology (machinery without fixed connection between the operating unit and the object of labor, semiautomatic machinery, automatic machinery) complained most often about working conditions (dirt, noise, heat). Workers doing manual labor complained about the difficulty of manual labor and about not working in the area for which they have been trained; automatic machine operators were content with the considerable physical stress.

The distribution of the different kinds of labor with regard to the percentage of workers who would have liked to leave their jobs immediately is interesting. This percentage was 17.4% among workers using manual instruments, 23.9% among workers using mechanized or electrical instruments, 22.8% among workers operating machines without fixed connection

between the operating unit and the object of labor, 25% among
workers on semiautomatic machinery, 20% among workers on
automatic assembly lines, and 6.7% among workers operating
machinery with programmed control.

At the present time (according to the results of our study)
the above-indicated instruments of labor are distributed as
follows (in percent): [3]

machinery with programmed control	0.4
automatic units or machines	3.4
manual instruments or simple devices	1.7
machinery without fixed connection between operating unit and object of labor	28.8
mechanized or electrical instruments	64.2
semiautomatic machinery	1.5

An extremely important issue is how this picture should look
by 1980 in order for all workers to be as completely satisfied
with their jobs as possible. In other words, in what direction
should technological progress develop in machine building in
order to achieve complete satisfaction of workers' intellectual
needs in the content of their labor? At issue here are the social requirements of technological progress and providing everyone with the kind of work he or she will like.

First, we must know the composition of the work force in
1980 with respect to our classification. This is quite difficult,
since data on age and sex could be obtained only from the 1959
census statistics. But even persons born in 1959 will be 21
years old in 1980, while a considerable proportion of the youth
will begin working at the age of 16 or 17. Hence it is necessary
to take into account the number of persons who were not yet
born in 1959. In addition, we still do not know whether the requirements of the law on universal secondary education will
be met. Hence our calculations can only be very rough.

We proceeded from the premise that even under conditions
of universal secondary education, only some portion of pupils
(even if the largest portion) will receive their education in a
daytime general education school and hence will move into the

factories with secondary education. Another portion will receive their education in evening higher educational institutions and correspondence schools and secondary specialized schools while they are working in the factories. The relative proportions of men and women among workers in the machine-building industry was assumed to be constant, since we have no data on possible changes in this regard. Estimates of the different age groups were made by shifting the current age composition ten years ahead, taking into account changes in the relative proportions of younger and older generations in our population by 1980.

Estimated Distribution of Workers in the Machine-Building Industry in 1980 by Groups (%)

1. Men under 30 with first- to seventh-grade education	0.3
2. Women under 30 with first- to seventh-grade education	0.2
3. Men under 30 with eighth- to ninth-grade education	4.5
4. Women under 30 with eighth- to ninth-grade education	3.7
5. Men under 30 with tenth-grade education and higher	13.4
6. Women under 30 with tenth-grade education and higher	13.1
7. Men 30 to 45 with first- to seventh-grade education	3.9
8. Women 30 to 45 with first- to seventh-grade education	2.5
9. Men 30 to 45 with eighth- to ninth-grade education	5.6
10. Women 30 to 45 with eighth- to ninth-grade education	3.4
11. Men 30 to 45 with tenth-grade education and higher	6.9

12. Women 30 to 45 with tenth-grade education
and higher   7.7
13. Men over 45 with first- to seventh-grade
education   21.2
14. Women over 45 with first- to seventh-grade
education   10.3
15. Men over 45 with eighth- to ninth-grade
education   0.9
16. Women over 45 with eighth- to ninth-grade
education   0.4
17. Men over 45 with tenth-grade education and
higher   1.3
18. Women over 45 with tenth-grade education
and higher   1.5

From the data presented here it is clear that the work force
will have become considerably older (the percentage of workers over 45 is not now very high owing to the demographic consequences of the war), and the level of education will increase.
The proportion of workers with a secondary education or more
will rise from 27.7% to approximately 44% by 1980.

Let us estimate the percentage of those instruments of labor
that workers in the different groups will be using, assuming
a positive attitude toward their work (Table 2, p. 41).

On the basis of the forecasts of the number and percentage
of members of the different typological groups among workers
in 1980, it is easy to calculate that for the maximum satisfaction of workers' intellectual needs in their work and for the
creation of optimal job attitude among workers, the following
distribution of the instruments of labor will be necessary by
1980 (in %):

manual instruments   20.7
machines without fixed connection between operating
   unit and object of labor   20.6
mechanized or electrical instruments   19.1
semiautomatic machinery   12.5
automatic units or machinery (except machinery

Table 2

Optimal Model of Distribution of Different
Kinds of Instruments of Labor by Typological Groups of Workers

Typological groups of workers	Manual instruments	Machines without fixed connection between operating unit and object of labor	Mechanized or electrical instrument	Semiautomatic machinery	Automatic units or machines	Machines with programmed control	Total
Men under 30, 1-7–grade education	7.1	18.0	20.8	30.7	23.4	–	100
Women under 30, 1-7–grade education	31.5	19.2	17.8	–	31.5	–	100
Men under 30, 8-9–grade education	20.3	12.6	13.5	16.1	17.2	20.3	100
Women under 30, 8-9–grade education	21.6	16.7	14.1	28.6	19.0	–	100
Men under 30, 10-grade education	–	19.1	20.1	13.2	25.5	22.1	100
Women under 30, 10-grade education	10.8	22.8	21.5	14.2	30.7	–	100
Men 30-45, 1-7–grade education	12.4	15.9	15.1	20.5	15.6	20.5	100
Women 30-45, 1-7–grade education	25.1	19.7	18.3	14.7	22.2	–	100
Men 30-45, 8-9–grade education	8.4	23.7	16.9	–	22.4	28.6	100
Women 30-45, 8-9–grade education	25.1	11.1	13.6	25.1	25.1	–	100
Men 30-45, 10-grade education	20.4	10.2	15.2	20.4	13.4	20.4	100
Women 30-45, 10-grade education	31.1	18.7	19.0	31.1	–	–	100
Men over 45, 1-7–grade education	31.3	27.3	22.6	–	18.8	–	100
Women over 45, 1-7–grade education	23.5	20.1	18.7	14.2	23.5	–	100
Men over 45, 8-9–grade education	34.7	37.1	38.2	–	–	–	100
Women over 45, 8-9–grade education	50.0	50.0	–	–	–	–	100
Men over 45, 10-grade education	20.0	40.0	40.0	–	–	–	100
Women over 45, 10-grade education	100	–	–	–	–	–	100

with programmed control)   19.6
machinery with programmed control   7.5

Such are the real social requirements for technology that
must be met in order to eliminate the contradiction between
the content of work and the level of education and in order to
achieve a good work attitude in each worker. Of course, economic and technological conditions will modify this distribution
to some extent; but in carrying out technological policy in machine building, we must take into account these sociopsychological needs. Otherwise, as the educational level of the work
force grows, work attitudes will deteriorate due to an inadequate intellectual content of work. [4]

Notes

1. It is not clear, in this connection, what form of movement
of labor their departure from their place of work would take:
labor turnover, social mobility, or movement associated with
technical progress.

2. Sotsial'nye issledovaniia, issue 2, Moscow, "Nauka"
Publishers, 1968, p. 83.

3. It should be noted that by no means all of those questioned
indicated the grade of implements of labor with which they
worked. Moreover, we could not classify a number of implements, especially imported ones, which are not familiar to
specialists. Hence we show here the distribution of implements of labor among 5,000 rather than 15,000 workers. Above
all, of course, individuals employed in simple manual labor
did not indicate their implements of labor. Thus the picture
of distribution of implements of labor is not altogether precise.
In reality manual labor and work on semiautomatic machines
make up a considerably larger share.

4. This problem is elucidated in the monograph, Chelovek
i ego rabota (Moscow, "Mysl'" Publishers, 1967), to which
we refer the reader.

3 WORK SATISFACTION: AN ANALYSIS OF EMPIRICAL GENERALIZATIONS AND AN ATTEMPT AT THEIR THEORETICAL INTERPRETATION

V. A. Iadov and A. A. Kissel'

One of the necessary aspects of research in the sociology of labor is an analysis of workers' satisfaction with the nature, content, and organization of their work, the study of the variety of factors influencing job satisfaction, and finally, the attempt to establish a connection between the state of satisfaction and the real behavior of a worker in production. Numerous studies conducted in this area in different countries have yielded quite different results.

There is nothing surprising in the fact that these studies disclose substantial differences in the nature and content of the needs of different social groups in one or another country, especially when data obtained in socialist and capitalist economies are compared, inasmuch as the different systems determine the mode of life of the population, what they require of their jobs, and how they go about meeting these requirements.

It should also not be surprising that an extremely variegated picture of the indices reflecting the "general level" of work satisfaction has been obtained in studies conducted at the same

From Sotsiologicheskie issledovaniia, 1974, no. 1, pp. 78-87. Translated by Michel Vale.

enterprise at a given time: indices of general work satisfaction, especially satisfaction with different aspects of work and with the production situation, are very sensitive to variations in individual needs and to the changing conditions of activity.

A difficult problem encountered by everyone studying this area is that there is no unique and unequivocal connection between the level of work satisfaction and the actual behavior of a worker in production under any given set of social conditions and for any given particular form of organization of production.

Indeed, this latter circumstance has created a real crisis situation in research into work and job satisfaction. If indeed the many "measures" of satisfaction are not correlated with the actual behavior of a worker in production (his productivity, conscientiousness, responsibility on the job, etc.), what is the sense of such measurements and are they really of any scientific or practical value?

Many sociologists in the United States and other capitalist countries working in this area have taken a narrow applied or managerial approach to the problem. They have renounced theory construction and concentrate exclusively on the accumulation of factual data relative to the situational behavior of different categories of workers in different aspects of productive activity.[1] This approach is completely understandable in the technocratic view of things, since in the final analysis what is important is the practical result, not the elucidation of the patterns that led to those results.

It is our view, however, that the proper approach to the problem must be sought in the development of an appropriate theoretical framework that provides a sufficiently thorough elucidation of the actual essence of the processes being studied. Only in such a case will the practical activities of managing production be given a reliable orientation. In particular, such a theory should inform practice; it should reveal what aspects of the organization of labor can be transferred from one sphere of labor activity to another; what aspects require a careful adaptation to the special features of production that differ from those in which they first proved effective, and which ones are totally unsuited for such borrowing. This is especially true in comparing data obtained from different social systems.

Before we turn to a theoretical examination of the problem, let us examine some facts illustrating, as we have already observed, the highly contradictory picture existing in this area.

Most contradictory are the indices showing the relationship between work satisfaction and the actual productivity of labor. According to the data from twenty studies conducted in the United States and generalized by V. Vroom, the average coefficient of correlation here was 0.14, with fluctuations between 0.86 to − 0.31, [2] which was close to the findings we obtained in a study of young Leningrad workers in 1963, where the corresponding coefficient was also 0.14.[3]   At the same time, F. Herzberg and others, comparing the results of twenty-six studies in the United States, found a positive association in fourteen cases, a negative association in three cases, and a lack of association in nine of the studies.[4]   I. Popova, studying workers in Odessa in 1970-73, found a weak but significant association in this relationship;[5] but according to some of her other findings, such an association did not exist.[6]

In the domain of creative work, especially in science, a positive association has been found between work satisfaction and high productivity.[7]

An association between the level of job satisfaction and discipline on the job is clear-cut, as has been pointed out by Soviet investigators[8] as well as by those studying the problem in capitalist enterprises.[9]

Finally, a definite inverse relationship has been found between the level of satisfaction and labor turnover. According to Popova, the coefficient of correlation is −0.60, with turnover much higher among these who are dissatisfied with work than among those who are satisfied.[10]   Investigators in the United States have found a rather high degree of association between job satisfaction and labor turnover under conditions of full employment, and a weakening of this association during an economic recession.[11]

Thus the closest associations are found between indices of

general work satisfaction, on the one hand, and discipline and stability of the work force, on the other. With regard to the productivity of labor, because of the many variables not considered in these studies (differences in incentive techniques, the rigor of supervision over the performance of job duties, the degree of identification of the worker with the production organization, etc.), the index of general work satisfaction in itself does not tell us very much.

Interpretations of data based on partial, mainly psychological mechanisms for the regulation of human behavior are no less contradictory than the data themselves.

Thus some American writers identify work satisfaction with the content of social attitudes toward various elements in the production situation or toward the job as a whole.[12]   But as R. Williams and F. Blackler justly point out, [13] such a view does not facilitate analysis of data bearing on the relationship between work satisfaction and behavior, but rather considerably impedes it. It is sufficient to point out that the regulatory functions of social attitudes are themselves in need of careful study and fundamental clarification. [14]

A Soviet investigator, A. Murutar, noted another point:[15] that work satisfaction was to a considerable extent correlated with a worker's view of the opportunities for fulfilling certain needs, and not only with the actual fulfillment of these needs. At a general psychological level this conclusion is similar to that of J. Thibout and H. Kelley, [16] who noted that a worker's stability in a particular organization was related not so much to his general level of satisfaction as to the existence of alternatives associated with the possibility of satisfying his interests by moving to another organization, as well as to differences in the "incentive value" of these alternatives. It follows that the general level of satisfaction or dissatisfaction should be related not only to a worker's attitude toward the particular organization but also to his attitude toward the opportunities for fulfilling his needs by shifting to another organization.

Finally, some writers claim that satisfaction is the result of success and achievement in actual productive activity,[17] while others see satisfaction as a prerequisite for such success.[18]

It is our view that the explanation for all of these facts must be sought not at the general psychological level but in socio-psychological concepts that encompass both social and general psychological mechanisms of the regulation of the social behavior of the individual.

First of all, let us note that in itself the comparison of levels of work satisfaction and the actual behavior of the worker in production can be neither understood nor used for forecasting a worker's activity in production without considering the specific social conditions that provide the context for these facts.

The problem of work satisfaction and its influence on a worker's actual behavior in an organizational system must be seen in the context of the concrete historical and social conditions of human activity, with due regard for the specific circumstances surrounding the decisions a worker makes and the specific needs of the individual.

In its most general form satisfaction is a psychological condition that occurs as the result of the fulfillment of some need dominant in the given relationship or social situation.

It is important to stress that the content of needs is directly determined by the social conditions under which the personality develops and by the conditions of work activity. Whatever particular scientific concept of a structure of needs we may use, the satisfaction of these needs is essentially a process of man's assimilation of some form of activity that is itself determined by social development.[19] Consequently, the multitude of social factors that determine the state of work satisfaction reflect objective conditions of labor activity within the system of needs of an individual who is, indeed, the subject of labor activity.

However, the source of motivation for behavior is often not the need itself but some "surrogates" for it, i.e., various individual predispositions toward perceiving a situation in a particular way, wherein these predispositions regulate the individual's behavior; in other words, they are personal dispositions that have become fixed in the individual's personality structure on the basis of specific needs. Because man learns repeatedly to satisfy certain needs in certain social situations, social orientations and other dispositional factors become fixed in the structure of his attitudes and relationships to the real world. Where a customary activity situation is repeated, a person's behavior is motivated no longer by a need as such but by a "surrogate" for it in the form of the corresponding disposition.[20]

Like needs, dispositions constitute a hierarchical system. The bases for such a hypothesis are to be found in studies of the role of value orientations, the general bent of an individual's personality, and the functions of social attitudes in the regulation of behavior.

We can assume that all of these factors are structured so that at the border line between elementary psychophysiological needs and the elementary conditions under which they can be satisfied are to be found dispositions to elementary behavioral acts: at the border line between deeper social needs associated with group activity and under the corresponding group conditions necessary for their satisfaction are formed social attitudes toward various social objects and situations. The need for creativity and self-actualization as one of the higher social needs of the individual is projected into a certain sphere of activity to which the individual ties his own major interests; in this way the general direction of interests becomes defined. Finally, value orientations that represent a selective attitude toward the basic goals of life activity and toward the means for achieving them, and result, moreover, from a clash between higher social needs and the general social conditions that both shape them and create the possibilities for their realization, form a higher level of dispositional structure.

A worker's behavior in a production situation, like man's social behavior in general, is regulated not by some sort of situational need taken in isolation but by the entire system of his dispositions and his attitude toward the general social and economic conditions of his activity, as well as toward the specific conditions of that activity. Only if this is realized will we be able to explain the aforementioned discrepancies in the

empirical findings and find a more adequate way to forecast
production activity, and hence to regulate behavior in the sphere
of work.

Let us see how the incentive role of various dispositions,
taken at different levels, manifests itself.

The decisive role is played by the higher dispositional levels:
namely, the system of value orientations of the individual, which
reflects primarily the social and economic conditions of labor
and of people's general life activities, the general ideological
atmosphere in which the individual's personality is shaped, and
then the nature of occupational activity, the specific circumstances surrounding the job itself, or the tasks entailed by a
particular occupation.

With regard to general social and cultural conditions, as
most objective observers of the bourgeois mode of life have
noted, the paramount importance of consumer orientations,
withdrawal into private life, and alienation in the domain of
work are the dominant characteristics of the social typology
of members of the "middle layers" and of part of the working
class. It is no accident that work satisfaction under these conditions is not correlated with general satisfaction with one's
life situation, [21] since work in bourgeois society in general
does not embrace the basic vital needs of the individual and is
regarded by him or her for what it actually is, a means for
existence, a means for realizing needs that have nothing to do
with the work one does in one's occupation.

It is quite revealing that in systematic studies of the hierarchy of value orientations of different groups of the population in the United States, one of the most well-known bourgeois
sociologists in this area, M. Rokeach, after carefully examining a list of values (and discarding more than three fourths of
those originally selected), in the end did not include work
among the meaningful human values. Ultimately the list was
left with thirty-six terms such as "material comfort," "life,
full gratification," "a quiet life," "internal harmony," etc.,
all directly related to an individualistic orientation or to a re-
treat into personal problems. Of broadly social values, the

author named "equality," "freedom," "happiness," "true friendship," etc. [22]

Soviet sociologists, on the other hand, have always pointed out the important role of a value orientation toward interesting and meaningful work among different social groups of the population, especially among young people. Thus according to the findings of mass surveys conducted among youth by V. T. Lisovskii, getting interesting work ranked highest among the career plans of young people. [23]   According to the findings of experimental surveys of workers and engineers (middle-aged men), conducted in Leningrad by V. V. Vodzinskaia, work ranked in first place in a list of nine values among engineers, and in second place on the list (after an orientation toward the family) among workers, while the value of "material satisfaction" was in fourth or fifth place in both groups. A large-scale survey of 1,000 engineers in designing and drafting organizations put work in third place out of eighteen possible values, along with orientation toward the family (general political values and health occupied the first two places); in these surveys material security ranked fifth or sixth (the average age of the men and women studied was 32).

The leading role of general social conditions of work emerges most clearly in comparisons of results of studies carried out using the same procedure on analogous groups of workers in the USSR and the USA. It was found that substantive interest in one's work (variety, possibility of making use of one's aptitudes and knowledge) ranked in first place in the hierarchy of motives of satisfaction or dissatisfaction with one's job among Soviet workers, while under conditions of capitalist production these motives played a secondary role behind such factors as confidence in job stability (i.e., a guarantee against unemployment) and the level of wages. [24]

The dispositional level closest to the system of value orientations is the general direction of an individual's interests, particularly (bearing in mind the question of interest to us) the level of identification of the worker with his occupation and his job.

According to our findings, as well as those of other investigators, identification with one's occupation or job increases substantially with the creative opportunities it offers and, of course, as a function of the level of responsibility borne for the activity of a large collective of workers. For example, among young workers in Leningrad studied in 1964, the dominant direction of interests was in work for 8%, as against 40%, mostly newlyweds, who were oriented toward the family, and 23% who were oriented toward education. [25] Among middle-aged engineers an explicit orientation toward one's occupational activity was found in 20% of those surveyed, with this percentage increasing with a rise in the degree of responsibility (the percentage of those who identified deeply with their job was much higher among the higher-level specialists than among practicing engineers). In mass surveys of scientific workers conducted by S. A. Kugel' (Leningrad), only 10-12% of those questioned were dissatisfied with the occupation they had chosen, while over 50% identified very deeply with their occupational activity.

Different elements in the production situation assume different personal meaning and hence have different motivational force depending on the degree of involvement in work. Psychological experiments have shown that the degree of involvement in a situation (in our case in the sphere of occupational acitvity) is directly related to the "predictive force" of social attitudes in their relationship to the subject's behavior. [26]

Finally, at the level of social attitudes toward specific conditions of work and toward the content of work activity, which in one way or another reflect the influence of higher dispositional levels of the personality (the system of value orientations and the general direction of the individual's interest), differences have universally been found in the evaluations of various elements of a production situation by men and women, young workers and older workers, workers with a high and with a lower level of skills, etc. [27]

In practical terms the interaction of all dispositional levels regulating the social behavior of the individual is determined

not only by the integral structure of the personality but primarily by the fact that this integrity is a reflection of the entire
system of objective conditions shaping the personality and determining its activity.

In objective reality itself the general and specific characteristics of labor activity function as a unity in an inseparable
connection with one another.

Thus the organization of production in a socialist enterprise
by no means may be regarded apart from the social and economic system taken as a whole, just as the organization of production in a capitalist enterprise reflects the entire range of
properties of the capitalist mode of production and distribution.
For example, in the organization of mangement in a socialist
enterprise, we find that in addition to the purely administrative
level of management, there is also a system of workers' supervision over the activity of the administration. This includes
supervision through the trade unions, the special administrative body — the PDPS (the Permanent Production Conference,
with workers constituting the majority), and the supervision of
the Communist Party organization in the particular enterprise
(in which most are also workers). The presence of these social institutions cannot help but affect the overall system of
management, work incentives, and the attitudes of the enterprise's personnel toward their jobs. For example, a study of
workers at enterprises in Tataria showed a significant association (0.25) between workers' participation in the management
of production and the productivity of their labor on the job.[28]
Hence attempts to translate the experience of management of
production in socialist enterprises into the terms of management of production in bourgeois society, and conversely the
attempt to draw on the experience of management of an industrial enterprise of some Italian or French firm and use it in
the practice of organization of production on the Volga or in
Tallin, is a question requiring careful study, both from the
standpoint of the socioeconomic nature of the overall social
system, into which only some of the elements of managerial
practice used in another social system may be "incorporated,"

as well as from the standpoint of the properties of the person-
alities of the workers themselves, which reflect the general
social and specific conditions of their labor activity.

In summary, we may conclude that, in itself, the measurement of the degree of work satisfaction provides merely an indication of the degree of a worker's adaptability to a particular
organization and nothing more. [29]   However, knowing this, a
sociologist is already able to explain and predict quite a bit.

If we take the degree of a worker's adaptability as the assimilation of the occupational and organizational requirements associated with his labor activity, then for purposes of theoretical
and practical interpretation of these findings, we can turn to
an analysis of the organization itself and the requirements it
imposes on the worker in his occupational or job position. Then
we shall be evaluating these general and specific requirements
rather than the level of satisfaction with one's job or occupation in itself.

For example, in the study mentioned above of young workers
in Leningrad, the proportion of those satisfied with their jobs
did not exceed 20% among unskilled or low-skilled workers,
while among workers doing highly skilled work involving the
operation or adjustment of automatic equipment, work satisfaction was about 50%. According to the findings of a study of
design engineers and draftsmen, the proportions fully satisfied
with their work were about 20% among rank-and-file engineers,
52.7% among group leaders, and 62% among higher-level specialists. The increase in the creative potential of a job, its
prestige, its pay (and among workers the average pay for low-
skilled work and heavy physical labor is even higher than it is
for workers employed on automatic equipment) provide some
idea of the content of the needs and dispositions realized in
work.

As for the relationship between the level of satisfaction and
the actual behavior of the worker on the job, in accordance
with the conception presented above, we must consider the entire system of dispositions. Attempts to find agreement between particular social orientations toward specific objects

and situations in productive activity and the degree of satisfaction measured in terms of specific elements in the production
situation, on the one hand, and the real behavior of workers in
production, on the other, have been unsuccessful. Nor can it
be otherwise if we consider that the regulation of behavior is
done by the entire system of personal dispositions, and the
regulative "force" of any particular component of this system
will depend both on its place in the dispositional hierarchy and
on the concrete goal of activity.

Thus, for example, in studying the behavior of an engineer
in a planning and drafting organization, we have distinguished
the following series of variables: (a) the system of requirements imposed on the engineer by the management and his col-
leagues — a content analysis of the certificates of competence
for the given group of engineers; (b) the system of dispositions
of the subjects being surveyed, including the hierarchy of basic
value orientations, the general direction of their interest in
work, leisure time and family, etc., their social attitudes toward different situations of productive activity under the particular conditions and over the long term; (c) the level of satisfaction with job or occupation and with different aspects of
the production situation; and (d) the individual's actual behavior
as evaluated by third parties. [30]

A content analysis should be made of the nature of the demands placed on the worker (for example, to be innovative,
creative, responsible, punctual, etc.) and the nature of his own
dispositions (the direction of his interests in work, given a
clearly pronounced orientation toward creativity and initiative,
or on the other hand, a general direction of interests outside
of his occupational activities, given a pronounced orientation
toward responsibility, punctuality, etc.). If there is a high
level of satisfaction with job and occupation, and if an orientation toward creativity in an engineer's work is combined with
an analogous structure of requirements imposed on an engineer
by his organization, we can predict a high level of effectiveness
and productivity in his behavior in production. Failure to adapt
to these requirements (low degree of satisfaction and pronounced

orientation toward executing orders) is a basis for predicting that the worker will be ineffective in the given organization (or given job). We will obtain the same result when we relate the disposition toward executing orders, combined with analogous requirements from the organization, and a high degree of work satisfaction (i.e., a high level of productivity for the given worker).

A low degree of satisfaction (lack of adaptation to the organization) together with a rather high level of productivity is also possible. However, this condition cannot continue (it is unstable) and one should expect either changes in the dispositional structure of the personality, or a decrease in the effectiveness of the worker, or the application of efforts to reorganize the organization itself, which is possible in certain cases (for example, in the area of science and management), or finally, the worker's departure from the particular organization. In that case one may presume that the resolution of the contradiction will depend on: (a) the level of coordination within the dispositional system of the personality; (b) the nature of the dominant direction of interests; and (c) some individual psychological characteristics of the subject, particularly his volitional potential and his intelligence. If the elements of an individual's dispositional system are poorly coordinated, there will be a shift toward an increase in the degree of satisfaction regardless of the state of the two other variables (a shift toward a higher level of adaptation to working conditions). If there is a high degree of coordination of the dispositional elements, but the dominant direction of the individual's interests lie outside the sphere of work, one can expect a high level of productivity with a low level of job satisfaction. Finally, if there is adequate coordination of the elements of the dispositional system, and the general direction of interests lies within the sphere of work, the outcome will depend on the psychological characteristics of the subject. There is reason to assume that a diminished volitional potential and rather high indices for intelligence (i.e., the individual's general adaptability to the conditions of his activity) will result in a reduction in his effectiveness in production or his move to a different job.

We have examined some hypotheses derived from our original conception, the chief content of which may be summed up as follows.

— Work satisfaction is the result of the coordination of a system of needs and/or their surrogate dispositions (dispositions toward a certain perception of social conditions and toward a certain kind of behavior fixed in the structure of the personality) with a subjective evaluation of the real possibilities of fulfilling these needs and/or dispositions.

— The level of work satisfaction is an index of the level of a worker's adaptation to the given production organization, i.e., of how the demands made on him and the opportunities offered to him correspond to his needs and orientations, his social attitudes, and the direction of his interests.

— Sociological analysis should focus not on the measurement of the level of work satisfaction as such but on (1) study of the demands made on the worker and the possibilities offered to him; (2) study of the characteristics of his dispositional system, in which it is desirable to ascertain the general direction of his interests, the dominating orientations toward goals in his life's activity, and finally, the social attitudes toward the significant elements in the production situation.

— Since a worker's behavior is regulated by his overall system of dispositional structures, the possibility of predicting his actual behavior in production on the basis of changes in his level of satisfaction will depend directly on the extent to which the leading components in this system are distinguished at the level of value orientations, general direction of interests (level of identification with his occupational activity and with the particular organization), and the social attitudes generated by them toward significant elements of the production situation: satisfaction associated with these leading components should have a relatively high "force," while satisfaction associated with peripheral aspects of the dispositional system (with respect to production activity and only in this respect) will not have such "force."

— The domination of one set of components or another in the dispositional system is determined in the first place by the general social conditions (socioeconomic, sociocultural, and sociopolitical), the nature and content of work, and finally, by individual characteristics of the worker's personality. This sequence of dominant premises — general social conditions, the nature of work, and individual personality features — should be taken into account in making a comparative analysis of empirical data derived from a study of the influence of work satisfaction on the actual behavior of the individual in production.

Notes

1. F. Blackler and R. Williams, "People's Motives at Work," in Peter B. War, ed., Psychology at Work, Penguin Books, 1971, pp. 294-309.

2. V. H. Vroom, Work and Motivation, New York, Wiley, 1964, p. 183.

3. A. G. Zdravomyslov, V. A. Rozhin, and V. A. Iadov, eds., Chelovek i ego rabota, Moscow, 1967, p. 137.

4. F. Herzberg, B. Mausner, R. O. Peterson, and D. F. Capwell, Job Attitudes: Review of Research and Opinion, Pittsburgh, Psychological Services of Pittsburgh, 1957, p. 199.

5. I. M. Popova, "Sotsiologicheskie problemy upravleniia sotsial'noi deiatel'nost'iu (na opyte konkretno-sotsiologicheskikh issledovanii v proizvodstvennykh kollektivakh)," dissertation for Doctor's Degree in Philosophical Sciences, Odessa, 1963, pp. 261-63.

6. Problemy sotsial'nogo regulirovaniia na promyshlennykh predpriiatiiakh, Kiev, 1973, p. 70.

7. D. Pel'tz and F. Endrius, Uchenye v organizatsiiakh, Moscow, 1973, pp. 195-201.

8. Problemy, p. 70.

9. Vroom, p. 178

10. Popova, p. 270.

11. Vroom, Work and Motivation, p. 178.

12. V. H. Vroom, "Industrial Social Psychology," in The
Handbook of Social Psychology, J. Lindsey and E. Aronson,
eds., vol. 5, London, 1968, pp. 198-204.
13. Williams and Blackler, p. 308.
14. M. Fishbein, "Attitude and the Prediction of Behavior,"
in M. Fishbein, ed., Readings in Attitude and Measurement,
New York, 1967; M. Y. McGuire, "The Nature of Attitudes and
Attitude Change," in The Handbook of Social Psychology,
J. Lindsey and E. Aronson, eds., vol. 3, London, 1968; Tittle
and R. Hill, "Attitude Measurement and Prediction of Behavior," Sociometry, vol. 30, 1967.
15. A. Murutar, "Opyt primeneniia faktornogo analiza pri
izuchenii lichnostnoi udovletvorennosti," Tezisy II Mezhdu-
narodnogo kollokviuma po sotsial'noi psikhologii, Tbilisi, 1970.
16. J. W. Thibout and H. H. Kelley, The Social Psychology
of Groups, New York, Wiley.
17. Zdravomyslov, Rozhin, and Iadov, p. 137.
18. L. W. Porter and E. E. Lawler, Managerial Attitudes
and Performance, Homewood, Ill., Richard D. Irwin, 1968.
19. K. Marx and F. Engels, The German Ideology, Sochine-
niia, vol. 3, p. 27.
20. L. A. Kiknadze, "K voprosu o sisteme faktorov povedeniia
cheloveka," Sotsiologicheskie issledovaniia, Tbilisi, 1971, p.
104.
21. J. Handyside and M. Speak, "Job Satisfaction: Myths and
Realities," British Journal of Industrial Relations, 1964, no. 1.
22. M. Rokeach, "Attitude Change and Behavioral Change,"
Public Opinion Quarterly, 1967, vol. 30.
23. V. T. Lisovskii, Eskiz k portretu, Moscow, 1969, p. 36.
24. V. A. Iadov, "Davaite smotret' faktam v litso," Voprosy
filosofii, 1965, no. 5.
25. Zdravomyslov, Rozhin, and Iadov, p. 249.
26. Pel'ts and Endrius, pp. 143-58; W. A. Scott, "Attitudes
Measurement," The Handbook of Social Psychology, J. Lindsey
and E. Aronson, eds., vol. 11, London, 1968, pp. 204-74.
27. N. A. Aitov, Nauchno-tekhnicheskii progress i dvizhenie
rabochikh kadrov, Moscow, 1972, pp. 75, 76; Sotsial'naia aktiv-

nost' rabotnikov promyshlennogo predpriiatiia, Kishinev, 1973, pp. 29-88; I. V. Nastavshev, "Otnoshenie k trudu i nekotorye kharateristiki lichnosti," in Lichnost' i problemy kommunisticheskogo vospitaniia, Voronezh, 1973; Zdravomyslov, Rozhin, and Iadov; Herzberg, Mausner, Peterson, and Carwell.

28. A. V. Tikhonov, "Soderzhanie i organizatsiia truda kak spetsificheskie faktory v protsesse formirovaniia otnosheniia k trudu," author's abstract of dissertation, Kazan, 1973, p. 22.

29. Another proof of this fact is to be found in data from a survey of about 2,000 workers on fishing vessels. Among those satisfied with their work, 49.8% were not inclined to change their job, while among those dissatisfied with their work, the figure was 23.3%; 18.2% of those satisfied with their work intended to change jobs, while 43.0% of those dissatisfied intended to do so. N. A. Sviridov, "Sotsial'naia adaptatsiia lichnosti v trudovom kollektiv," dissertation for the Degree of Candidate in Philosophy, Leningrad, 1974, p. 154.

30. This study is now being carried out by a team including V. Vodzinskaia, L. Doktorova, V. Kaiurova, A. Kissel', G. Saganenko, A. Semenov, and V. Iadov (head of project).

PUBLIC OPINION ON ELECTING MANAGERS

Ia. S. Kapeliush

Introduction

Purpose and Method of the Survey

On September 24, 1968, under the headline "Who Should be a Work Superintendent?" Komsomol'skaia pravda published "A Report on an Unusual Competition: a Captain of Production Is Elected." The report related how in one of our construction administrations, the Krasnoiarsk Aliuminstroi, a senior work superintendent was elected. He was elected in the same way a trade union committee or a candidate for deputy to a soviet is elected. Speeches were made, the candidates were discussed, and there was a vote. What was extraordinary about this event was that the senior work superintendent received his authority not from some higher level of command, as is the case with ordinary appointments, but from his subordinates.

The journalist reported that "in a few days a foreman will be elected. Then, in routine order, all work superintendents,

From Ia. S. Kapeliush, Obshchestvennoe mnenie o vybornosti na proizvodstve, Information Bulletin no. 39 (54) of the Institute of Empirical Social Research of the Academy of Sciences of the USSR, Moscow, 1969, pp. 4-24 and 95-97. Translated by Michel Vale.

foremen, and group leaders.... The experiment is being
watched attentively by public organizations and the trust administration, and party organs throughout the territory have
shown an interest in it. There is talk about extending the experiment and conducting similar elections in several industrial
enterprises in Krasnoiarsk."

This report attracted considerable attention among readers.
The editors received numerous letters discussing the merits
and shortcomings of the experiment and the possibilities and
consequences of extending it; various suggestions were made,
questions were raised, and issues were debated (see Komsomol'-
skaia pravda, October 8, 1966, and May 12, 1967). The Krasnoiarsk experiment had its successors: similar elections were
held in Baku (see the letter "The Effect of Confidence," Komsomol'skaia pravda, June 24, 1967). Other newspapers were
also interested in the experiment: Izvestia ("The Wrong Kind-
ness, Brigade Leader," July 16, 1967), Literaturnaia gazeta
("Simple Proceedings," October 4, 1967), and so on.

Public interest in the experiment is understandable. An economic reform is being carried out in the country, the essence
of which is to place stress on economic rather than administrative methods of management in industry, the return to such
important economic levers as profit, prices, bonuses, and cred-
its, the granting of more economic independence to enterprises,
and the broadening of the rights of enterprise employees. The
resolution of the September 1965 Plenary Session of the Central Committee of the Communist Party of the Soviet Union
laid the foundations for the reform; the resolution states that
the reform should "ensure the further extension of the democratic principles of management and create the economic pre-
conditions for the broader participation of the masses in the
management of production and for their influence on the results of the economic performance of an enterprise. This system of economic management more fully meets modern requirements and should enable the advantages of the socialist
system to be better utilized." [1]

But what does this mean in practice? What does it mean to

expand the rights and powers of all working people of an enterprise (both the management and the rank and file), transforming
them into genuine masters of their enterprise? For management this means freeing them from petty tutelage, the elimination of a situation in which all activity is reduced to carrying
out a steady stream of orders and regulations sent down from
above. Now enterprise managers have been given the opportunity to demonstrate their initiative and creativity in dealing
not only with day-to-day questions but long-run problems as
well. Now the responsibility rests with them to determine not
only the technological process, the technical equipment of an
enterprise, the state of working capital, but also the total number of employees, and even their pay. Rank-and-file workers
also have been given a broader basis for exercising their initiative. Now that they have material incentives, they are more
often included in the collective search for the most effective
methods and techniques of work, and they pay more attention
to and take better care of public property. But the changes in
the rights and powers involved in deciding fundamental questions have not been as great for the rank and file as for the
managerial staff. The economic reform, like other measures
and undertakings of the party and government in this area,
have of course been aimed at involving workers more exten-
sively in the management of production and in deciding on economic and other fundamental questions of an enterprise's operation. However, such goals cannot be achieved in one sharp,
sudden thrust or effort. It is a gradual process, and a long
one. Hence, while it is true that a broadening of economic independence for the enterprise automatically implies expanding
the powers of its management, rank-and-file workers will not
be able immediately to occupy a position that would allow them
to feel themselves to be the masters of their enterprise on an
equal footing with management. An imbalance sets in which
bears within it certain dangers. Once this imbalance has developed, it could have a negative effect on moral (and even
perhaps material) incentives, on which the effectiveness of
production has always depended. If workers are aware of this

imbalance, it will hardly be conducive to a growth in production or an improvement in the productivity of labor, etc.

The Krasnoiarsk and Baku experiments prevent the development of this imbalance. The enterprise staff — workers, technicians, engineers — are given the right to decide one of the most important questions of management: who is to be a manager. By participating in the elections of managers, each worker and engineer thereby receives an additional opportunity to exert a real influence on the life of his enterprise through the person of the elected manager. Moreover, the interest of the workers in an enterprise in the selection of the most capable management has not only a moral but also a material aspect. After all, the economic reform links the wages of each worker even more closely than before to the successful operation of his enterprise as a whole. Now a worker has a vital interest in having competent leaders managing his enterprise so that the enterprise reaps maximum profits and so that wages increase. It is also of interest to the government in general that enterprises should be managed by competent personnel: the higher the profits of an enterprise, the more funds flow from it to the state budget, and the greater the opportunities for improving the well-being of the people. In a word, there is a merging of the interests of each individual worker, the enterprise, and the state as a whole — the chief objective of the reform. On the other hand, the section of the resolution of the Plenary Session of the Central Committee that speaks about the further expansion of democratic principles of management has been given concrete form: elections to responsible managerial positions are one of the basic elements of democracy.

Noting the importance of the Krasnoiarsk and Baku experiments and the interest the newspaper articles aroused, the Sector for the Study of Public Opinion of the Department of Empirical Sociological Research of the Institute of Philosophy of the Academy of Sciences of the USSR[2] and the Public Opinion Institute of <u>Komsomol'skaia pravda</u> decided to ascertain the real attitude of the public to the question of elections of industrial managers and to conduct a countrywide survey on this question. After all, one can assume that journalists' reports and readers' letters reflect only the interests of a narrow circle of specialists.

The main purpose of the survey dictated a special approach to the study. The social relevance and novelty of the problem ruled out posing such general abstract questions as "How do you feel about electing industrial managers?" etc. It was more reasonable to measure the immediate reaction of different groups of the population to a particular, specific way of dealing with the problem, even the particular issue involved in the article in Komsomol'skaia pravda of September 24. Accordingly, each person interviewed was given reprints of the newspaper article entitled "Who Should Be a Work Superintendent?" and a questionnaire that referred to the content of this article. At the same time, this type of survey also enabled us to answer another question: to measure the response of Komsomol'skaia pravda readers to a particular newspaper article and to determine the impact of such an article.

The survey was conducted using the so-called method of stratified nonproportional sampling among those groups and layers (strata) of the population directly concerned with the particular problem, and whose opinion could therefore be assumed to have some social relevance. The number of representatives in each group was determined independently of the objective proportions characterizing the respective positions of the different groups in society. Thus the sample included the following (the number in the right-hand column represents the number of those questioned, while the letters in parentheses represent the code for each group):

1. Workers in industrial and construction enterprises
   (13 enterprises, 8 cities)   363 (W)

2. Workers-deputies of soviets,   105 (D)
   including:
   a) workers-deputies of municipal soviets
      (8 cities)   34
   b) workers-deputies of the Supreme Soviet of
      the USSR   71

3. Rank-and-file engineers and technicians —
   specialists having no direct subordinates
   (7 enterprises, 6 cities)   51 (E)

4. Lower-level managers — brigade leaders
   foremen, senior foremen, work superin-
   tendents (13 enterprises, 8 cities)   86 (L)

5. Higher-level managers,   84 (H)
   including:
   a) superintendents of shops, departments,
      and services   38
   b) directors, superintendents, and other
      managerial personnel in enterprises   46

6. Heads of public organizations,   114 (P)
   including:
   a) secretaries of party committees in
      enterprises   30
   b) secretaries and workers in the adminis-
      tration of Komsomol municipal committees   53
   c) chairmen and workers of the administrative
      apparatus of the regional trade union councils   31

7. Scientists and journalists,   97 (S)
   including:
   a) economists (chairmen and teachers in
      departments of economics and of the
      organization and planning of industry)   36
   b) philosophers, social scientists, lawyers
      (scientific workers and teachers)   31
   c) journalists (editors of local and journalists
      in central newspapers)   30

Total   900

Three groups of those just enumerated — the first (workers), the third (rank-and-file engineers and technicians), and the fourth (lower-level managers) — were questioned by survey-takers at the following enterprises:

1. Volgograd: the Krasnyi Oktiabr' Metallurgical Factory, the Volgograd Gidrostroi Trust;
2. Dzhankoi: the machine-building plant;
3. Kirov: the soil-cultivating machinery plant;
4. Moscow: the Likhachev Automobile Factory, the Mosstroi-1 Trust, the Baranochnyi Factory No. 1;
5. Novosibirsk: the leather shoe combine, the mechanical repair plant;
6. Saratov: the heavy machinery factory;
7. Sverdlovsk: the Sportobuv Factory;
8. Ussuriisk: the municipal food plant.

Thus the personnel survey covered 12 enterprises in 7 cities.

The other groups — worker-deputies, higher-level enterprise managers, heads of public organizations, scientists, and journalists — were surveyed by mail. A total of 1,600 questionnaires were sent out. One fourth of them, 400, were returned to the Komsomol'skaia pravda Public Opinion Institute. We can assume that the questionnaire-return ratio would have been higher on the whole if it had not been for one circumstance, namely, that the letters were sent out only ten days before the date for return indicated on the questionnaires. Over a month's time 122 questionnaires were returned, and on almost half of them was written the note: "questionnaire received too late." Evidently many of those surveyed simply did not risk going beyond the deadline and did not send back their answers. All were sent reminders, which helped us retrieve the remaining questionnaires.

The representativeness of each group was ensured by the size of the group and by a broad geographical dispersion. The survey included more than 50 cities in the Soviet Union. Table 1 provides a general picture of the sociodemographic structure of the surveyed groups.

It is readily understandable that a stratified nonproportional sample does not permit us to derive average figures characterizing public opinion as a whole. The findings of the survey only have meaning with regard to the answers of each particular group.

Table 1

Sociodemographic Structure of Those Surveyed

	Basic groups*						
	W	D	E	L	H	P	S
Total in group	363	105	51	86	84	114	97
Men	208	56	38	62	81	99	90
Women	155	49	13	24	3	12[a]	7
16-24 years	58	3	3	6	—	1	—
25-29 years	88	16	15	22	10	44	11
30-39 years	107	44	16	32	23	26	32
40-59 years	101	40	16	26	50	30	44
60 years and older	9	—	—	—	1	1	7
Less than 7 grades	96	2	—	4	—	2	—
7-9 grades	150	49	—	12	1	—	—
General secondary	98	41	3	20	9	16	1
Specialized secondary	—	7	21	35	19	26	1
Incomplete higher	19	4	2	3	8	6	2
Higher	—	—	24	10	47	50	93
Members of Communist Party	67	53	17	42	65	90	77
Members of Komsomol	65	6	10	12	2	5	2
Nonparty	216	40	15	21	7	3	6
On job less than one year	15	—	5	6	3	7	2
1-3 years	57	1	9	18	7	22	4
4-10 years	125	35	19	32	23	49	30
Over 10 years	155	67	15	28	49	12	57

*Editor's note: For the occupational groups designated by these letters, see pp. 64-65.

a) In this case, as in all others, the difference between the total number of those questioned in a group and the sum of its components is explained by the fact that some individuals did not indicate their vital statistics in the questionnaire (i.e., sex, age, etc.).

Position on the Main Question

The main questions on the questionnaire concerned the essence of the experiment: Is it appropriate to elect industrial
managers? Who should be elected? How should they be
elected? An analysis of the answers to these questions enabled
us to delineate the main position of each group surveyed.

1. Who Is For? Who Is Aganist?

The first question on the questionnaire was formulated as
follows: "Is it appropriate at the present time to make certain
managerial positions in production elective?"

The distribution of answers to this question (yes, no, it is
hard for me to say) is interesting (see Table 2).

The figures speak for themselves: in each group most of
those questioned supported the idea of elections to managerial
positions in industry. However, it is easy to see that attitudes
varied considerably from one group to another. Indeed, these
differences were sometimes even greater in subgroups. Thus
50.0% of directors of enterprises and 34.2% of shop superintendents (in the fifth group), 32.4% of trade union workers and
26.7% of secretaries of factory party committees (in the sixth
group), 30.5% of economists specializing in the organization
of production, 13.3% of journalists, and 3.2% of social scientists (in the seventh group), etc., thought that elections were
inappropriate.

A distinct pattern is evident: the greater the involvement
of the group in management of production, in particular, the
higher the position in the occupational hierarchy, the greater
the number of opponents to elections. This pattern was most
evident among participants in production. While among workers and rank-and-file engineers 1 in 10 was against elections,
the figures were 1 in 4 among foremen, 1 in 3 among shop superintendents, and even 1 in 2 among directors.

A similar picture was observed among scientists as well as
among heads of public organizations. Whereas social scien-

Table 2

Answers Concerning the Appropriateness of Elections at
the Present Time (in percent of number questioned)

Basic groups	Types of answers			No answer	Total
	yes	no	hard to say		
1. Workers	89.0	4.7	6.3	—	100.0
2. Worker deputies of soviets	82.9	6.6	8.6	1.9	100.0
3. Rank-and-file engineers	88.2	5.9	3.9	2.0	100.0
4. Lower-level managers	66.3	26.7	5.8	1.2	100.0
5. Higher-level managers	52.4	42.8	3.6	1.2	100.0
6. Heads of public organizations	77.2	19.3	1.7	1.8	100.0
7. Scientists and journalists	81.4	16.5	—	2.1	100.0

tists, who have no direct relation to the management of industry, almost unanimously favored elections, economists, who
not only teach the organization of industry to future shop superintendents and directors but themselves, as the questionnaires showed, had worked for many years in industry before
entering teaching, showed only one third in favor of elections.
While a total of 7.5% of Komsomol workers, who were only partially concerned with production in connection with the problems of working youth, were against elections, the percentage
was four times greater among trade union workers, who much
more frequently confront problems of production and very often
themselves previously worked in production. And so on.

But Table 2 in itself still does not allow us to conclude that
the differences in the positions of those questioned were re-

lated mainly to their socio-occupational status. Perhaps these
differences were due to other factors, such as age, education,
party membership, or sex? Unfortunately, the extremely small
size of some of the groups does not permit a thorough analysis,
but even a selective analysis has much to tell us.

From Table 3 it is apparent that age has a clear effect. In
six of the seven groups the number of those in favor of elections
decreases with increasing age. This pattern is especially evident in groups in which opponents of elections were relatively
numerous: namely, among managers of industry and heads of
public organizations. The variation here is as much as 20-24%.

But education does not play such a role. We were unable to
find any regular pattern here. The distribution of answers also
shows no systematic relationship to party membership and sex.
The variations here were not very great: in most cases they
did not exceed 5%

On the other hand, as Table 3 shows, when the main groups
are arrayed in order of decreasing number of supporters of
elections, the figures on each line decrease steadily in most
cases, showing very impressive variations, at times up to 46%.
This means that factors associated with the socio-occupational
status of those questioned play a decisive role. The attitude
people have to the idea of elections is related primarily to their
socio-occupational status and to the extent of their participation
in management.

2. Elected Positions

The general question of the appropriateness of elections had
a sequel: What specific positions can be made elective? This
question was posed in our questionnaire in "open" form, i.e.,
it was not accompanied by a set of possible answers. Those
questioned named the positions themselves. Their answers
can be grouped as follows:

1. Brigade leader (only).
2. Foreman, senior foreman, work superintendent, section
head, and other lower-level managers (direct organizers) in

Table 3

Number in Favor of Elections
(in percent of those questioned)

	Basic groups*						
	W	E	D	S	P	L	H
Average number in favor of elections in group	89.0	88.2	82.9	81.4	77.2	66.3	52.4
16-24 years old	94.8	—	—	—	—	—	—
25-29 years old	91.0	93.5	81.5	—	88.8	73.0	—
30-39 years old	87.9	87.8	84.0	87.6	77.0	59.5	61.0
40 years and above	87.0	87.8	80.0	76.7	64.6	65.4	41.2
Less than secondary education	87.0	—	94.2	—	—	56.1	—
Secondary general education	96.0	—	75.8	—	62.8	75.0	—
Secondary specialized and incomplete higher education	79.0	87.0	—	—	81.3	68.5	63.0
Higher education	—	91.8	—	80.8	82.0	—	49.0
Members of Communist Party	86.6	82.3	81.1	79.3	86.8	62.0	47.7
Nonparty	88.4	100.0	85.0	—	—	57.1	—
Men	89.4	86.8	82.1	81.0	75.8	67.9	53.1
Women	88.3	85.0	83.8	—	—	62.7	—

*See the chart on pp. 64-65.

production.

3. Chief engineer, chief designer, chief technologist, and other managerial personnel in production — technical specialists (including senior specialists).

4. Directors (superintendents, managers) of an enterprise, shop superintendents, section superintendents, and other higher-level managers in production (excluding those named in point 3).

5. Heads of departments of a ministry and other managerial

personnel in state administration.

6. All managerial jobs — from brigade leader to director and minister.

7. Head of a department of a scientific research institute, superintendent of a school, newspaper editor, and other leaders of nonproductive collectives.

On the whole this grouping (especially group 2) fully conforms to the existing structure of a socialist state productive enterprise.[3] Only group 6 constitutes a clear exception, since it includes vague, diffuse answers without the enumeration of any specific positions: "all positions having to do with the management of production can be elective," etc.

The distribution of answers in accordance with this grouping is shown in Table 4. As we see, those questioned named primarily lower-level managerial positions as elective. The number of such statements (including the job of brigade leader) in all groups of supporters of elections was never lower than 72%.

However, higher-level managerial positions were also often mentioned. In 5 of the 7 groups of persons questioned, the number of instances in which such positions were mentioned exceeded 14%, and in 3 groups it even exceeded 20%. On the other hand, managerial positions of technical specialists (designers, technologists, etc.) were named very rarely by all groups: only once did the figure for such jobs reach 6.8%.

Let us try to interpret these figures. The fact that those questioned named primarily jobs of brigade leader, foreman, and other lower-level managerial personnel does not require much explanation. These supervisors are at the lowest level of the managerial ladder; they are closest to the workers and are the direct organizers of production. In addition, the article in Komsomol'skaia pravda dealt specifically with these positions. As far as the other figures are concerned, they must be examined more carefully.

The activity of a present-day manager of production consists of two parts: management of the technological process and management of people. The choice of a candidate for such a leadership position and the evaluation of his activity are based

Table 4

Answers Concerning Which Positions Should Be Made
Elective (in percent of those favoring elections)

Basic groups	Types of answers							No answer
	1	2	3	4	5	6	7	
1. Workers	1.0	71.0	1.0	3.7	—	4.4	0.3	24.7
2. Worker-deputies to soviets	5.8	81.6	2.3	8.5	—	5.8	—	8.5
3. Rank-and-file engineers	15.6	66.9	—	15.6	—	8.9	—	11.1
4. Lower-level managers	24.6	58.0	—	3.5	—	3.5	—	12.2
5. Higher-level managers	29.6	61.5	6.8	18.2	2.3	9.1	—	—
6. Heads of public organizations	20.5	75.2	2.3	13.7	—	3.4	1.1	1.1
7. Scientists and journalists	5.1	71.9	3.9	12.8	—	9.0	5.1	12.8

on this division. For the correct management of the technological process, a specialized technical education is a primary
and absolute necessity. In addition there are quite precise criteria for the objective assessment of such management: the
quantity and quality of output, profitable utilization of energy
and technology, the use of the most productive methods, etc.
In other words, the assessment by the management of the technological process today is highly formalized. Thus the choice
of a person who will implement this activity most effectively
does not constitute a major difficulty.

But the assessment of the activity of managing people is
much less formalized. This is an area of dispute, a clash of
different points of view, a domain of "pure" public opinion. The
criteria for an objective assessment here are essentially absent. The question of who is the best manager is usually de-

termined on the basis of the subjective evaluations of people,
and such parameters as education, experience, etc., of both
the person doing the evaluating and the person being evaluated
are not of decisive importance. Everything depends on a number of highly individual characteristics of the person. Any
leader can be and is the object of the subjective evaluations of
both the workers under him as well as persons standing over
him. However, whereas the opinion of those above him plays
a decisive role in determing the appointment of someone to a
leadership position, if such a person is elected it is his subordinates whose evaluation is decisive.

What aspect dominates in the activity of a particular manager
of production: his activity in managing the technological process
or in managing people? Special studies are necessary for a
precise answer to this question. But if we compare groups of
leaders such as those involved in direct leadership and "line"
positions (foremen, shop superintendents, directors), on the
one hand, and those who are not in "line" leadership (technologists, designers, energy engineers), on the other, we can say
with certainty that the activity of the latter is basically the
management of the technological process. As already indicated,
the selection of a specialist for such a position may be made in
accordance with strictly objective criteria. This also should
explain why so few of those questioned were in favor of electing
"nonline" superiors (various kinds of technical specialist),
while many were in favor of electing immediate superiors.

This was confirmed in the answers of the respondents themselves. "All those who manage people should be elected,"
writes S. I., head of the Personnel Department at the Volga
Factory. "All those who are in close contact with workers
should be elected," says P. A., a journalist from Sverdlovsk.
"All those who are directly involved in managing people," adds
S. V., a teacher at Leningrad University. "Everyone who during the course of the working day supervises the correct performance of jobs, who helps or who teaches, or who is himself
constantly in the sight of the workers."

All these justifications (a total of 350 such statements appeared in the questionnaires of those favoring elections) can be classified into three general groups:

1. Positions basically involving the management of people should be elective.

2. Positions of managers who are closest to workers, who are in direct contact with them, should be elective.

3. Positions of managerial personnel whom the workers-electors could know personally should be elective.

The frequency of these answers on the questionnaires is shown in Table 5.

Table 5

Reasons for Making Certain Positions Elective
(in percent of total reasons)

Basic groups	Kinds of answers				Total
	1	2	3	Other	
1. Workers	15.7	46.5	18.9	18.9	100.0
2. Worker-deputies of soviets	15.4	61.7	17.2	5.7	100.0
3. Rank-and-file engineers	30.0	40.1	26.6	3.3	100.0
4. Lower-level managers	13.3	56.7	30.0	–	100.0
5. Higher-level managers	31.2	37.6	31.2	–	100.0
6. Heads of public organizations	11.9	59.6	21.4	7.1	100.0
7. Scientists and journalists	22.7	47.8	22.7	6.8	100.0

If we examine the positions that, according to those questioned, could be made elective (Table 4), we must not overlook those who named only positions of brigade leader. There were quite a few: in some groups more than 20%. It was necessary to determine whether those questioned thought that jobs above

brigade leader could be made elective. This was of fundamental
importance, since in many cases a brigade leader (especially
one who is not released from ordinary work duties) differs little
from a rank-and-file worker, and his leadership is only nominal. If those who named only brigade leaders were against making other positions elective, then they can more likely be considered as opposed to elections rather than in favor of them.

It was not difficult to clarify this matter. We found that most
of those in favor of electing brigade leaders shared a common
viewpoint: "Only brigade leaders who are not released from
basic work duties should be elected, since they do not have administrative powers" (P. Iu., factory director in Transbaikal).
Only rank-and-file engineers and scientists were an exception
to this.

Thus most of those who recognized the possibility of electing
brigade leaders nonetheless were basically against electing
managers of production. In summary, the number of opponents
of elections increases as follows: among higher-level managers
to 52.3%, among lower-level managers to 33.7%, among heads
of public organizations to 29.8%, among worker-deputies of soviets to 9.5%, and among workers to 5.5% (see Table 2, p. 69).

It is striking that the largest "increment" in the number of
opponents of elections occurs precisely in those groups that
previously had more opponents anyway. For higher-level managers the increment was 9.5%, for lower-level managers it
was 7.0%, for heads of public organizations — 10.5%

Nonetheless, despite the "increment" the overall distribution
of respondents with regard to the question of elections remained
as before: in all groups, except the group of enterprise directors and shop superintendents, the number of supporters of
elections considerably exceeded the number of opponents. At
this point it would be useful to return again to the answers to
the question of what positions should be elective (Table 4, p. 74).

We have already noted that in addition to lower-level managers, higher-level positions were also named, and not only in
each of the major groups but also in the subgroups: 34.4% of
social scientists, 31.8% of shop superintendents, 27.3% of en-

terprise directors, 25.0% of trade union workers, 24.5% of rank-and-file engineers, 20.0% of economists specializing in the organization of production, 14.9% of Komsomol workers, 14.3% of secretaries of party committees in factories, 14.3% of worker-deputies to the Supreme Soviet, 13.0% of worker-deputies to municipal soviets, 8.4% of journalists, 8.1% of workers, and 7.0% of lower-level managers. On the whole, in 10 of the 13 groups (counting the subgroups) the number of times higher positions were named exceeded 13%, and in 6 groups it was even as high as 20%.

But who is out in front? It would be reasonable to assume that representatives of groups in which the number of those favoring elections was on the whole higher would mention electing persons in higher positions more than others. Actually, however, as we can see from the figures just given, six of these "leaders" are quite different: four of these leaders — enterprise directors, shop superintendents, trade union workers, and economists — belonged in the ranks of those most actively opposed to elections.

The explanation for this paradoxical phenomenon — paradoxical at first glance — is to be found in the level of competence of the judgments offered by these groups. The higher the educational level (most of those questioned in these groups had finished higher educational institutions — see Table 1), and the greater the experience (almost half of those questioned in these groups had had more than 10 years on the job), the greater care they took and the more objective they were in examining the particular problem, and the more consistent were their arguments. Indeed, if in their opinion a foreman or a work superintendent could be elected, then what was the essential reason why higher-level managers should not also be elected? Having said "a," these people were more inclined than others to say "b."...

Conclusion

The problem of elections of managers of production is a rel-

atively recent one, since such a question can be posed only in
a society in which social ownership of the means of production
prevails and where the entire society rather than some part of
it controls production.

As Lenin said on the eve of the socialist revolution in defining
the tasks of the proletariat, "Universal election and replace-
ment of all persons in responsible positions seems merely on
the surface a measure of simply more complete democracy.
Indeed, this 'simply' makes a tremendous difference, in which
certain institutions are replaced by others of a fundamentally
different type. This is one of those cases where 'quantity is
transformed into quality.' Democracy, implemented to the full-
est and most consistent degree conceivable, transforms bourgeois democracy into proletarian democracy."[4]

"Socialization in fact," bringing into conformity social production and social control, cannot help but mean the election
of managers of production. "The masses must have the right
to elect for themselves their responsible leaders; the masses
must have the right to replace them; and the masses must have
the right to know and to check on every smallest step in their
activity. The masses must have the right to promote all their
working members without exception to administrative and ex-
ecutive functions."[5]

The problem of electing people to positions of management
has constantly been under the scrutiny of the Communist Party
of the Soviet Union. The Twenty-second Congress included
the following in the Third Party Program: "The principal of
elections and accountability to representative bodies and to the
electorate must be gradually extended to all persons of responsible leadership positions in state bodies."[6]

In the light of all this, one must agree with the opinion of one
of the participants in our survey, the Moscow engineer M. B.:
"Election of leaders is not an experiment but, according to
Marxist theory, a stage in the development of society. One can
experiment only with forms of implementation of elections."

However, the election of managers of production is thus far
no more than an unproved hypothesis. Science has not yet ac-

cumulated facts confirming the soundness or unsoundness of
this hypothesis. Arguments about the possible advantages or
disadvantages of elections have not gone beyond surmises and
conjectures. The election of managers of production remains,
as before, only a prerogative of public opinion.

Thus the accurate sounding of public opinion acquires a special significance in this connection. Indeed, in discussing such
problems, reference to public opinion has sometimes been the
only argument. Debates and polemics on this issue have taken
place at different stages of development of Soviet society.

Thus in 1957, in discussing the question of shifting industry
to a system of management based on economic councils, the
question of elections came up. One of the opponents of elections
objected to those who "wanted to shift from the system of appointment from above to elections from below of managerial
staffs of enterprises"; he pointed out with satisfaction that
"views of this sort were incidental and exceptional."[7] The results of our survey warrant the presumption that such views
were by no means exceptional.

The period after the Twenty-second Congress was marked
by a heightened discussion of this problem. Moreover, not only
opponents but supporters of elections have voiced unsubstan-
tiated arguments. Here is one of the freshest examples. One
of the questionnaires was returned to us with the following concluding comment: "I answered all your questions, but honestly
I did not understand why such a survey was necessary. It is
obvious beforehand that the reaction to the proposal will be
universally favorable and that it will be impossible to make
the election of managers a reality," D. V., philosophy teacher
in Moscow.

D. V. was wrong in her first assumption. Her mistake, like
the mistake of the earlier opponent of elections, was quite typical and clearly showed the groundlessness of such a priori
judgment regarding public opinion; it demonstrates the need
to constantly study public opinion.

As for D. V.'s second assumption, whether it is correct or
not will depend on the passage of time and, indeed, on the role

that public opinion will play in resolving this question.

Notes

1. On the Convocation of the Regular Twenty-second Congress of the Communist Party of the Soviet Union. On the Improvement of the Management of Industry, the Refinement of Planning, and the Intensification of Economic Incentives in Industrial Production. Resolutions of the Plenary Session of the Central Committee of the Communist Party of the Soviet Union, Adopted September 29, 1965, Politizdat, 1965, p. 11.

2. Today the Center for the Study of Public Opinion of the Institute of Empirical Social Research of the Academy of Sciences of the USSR.

3. Statute on Socialist State Enterprises, "Ekonomika" Publishers, 1965, p. 27.

4. V. I. Lenin, Poln. sobr. soch., vol. 33, p. 42.

5. Ibid., vol. 36, p. 157.

6. Proceedings of the Twenty-second Congress of the Communist Party of the Soviet Union, Moscow, Gospolitizdat, 1962, p. 399.

7. "Demokraticheskii tsentralizm — osnova upravleniia sotsialisticheskim khoziaistvom," Kommunist, 1957, no. 4, p. 10.

5 THE INTERRELATIONSHIP OF SOCIAL FACTORS DETERMINING WORK ATTITUDES

N. I. Alekseev

Collective fisheries are scattered throughout the entire country. In 1970 there were 536 of them in the Soviet Union. About
320,000 persons lived in these collectives, with 53,000 of them
being employed in the fishing industry, 35,000 in agriculture,
and 25,000 in subsidiary industries. In 1970 the collective fisheries were responsible for almost one fourth of the total catch,
as is also the case today. Despite their importance, collective
fisheries are still an unknown area for our economic and sociological science.

The postwar history of the collective fisheries can be divided
into three stages. The first was the stage of simple reproduc-
tion (from 1946 through 1954). The incomes of the fisheries
scarcely covered their expenses. The material base of this
period consisted of sailboats and rowboats, rarely equipped
with small motors. The work was manual. In 1950 the collective fishing industry employed 103,000 persons, who caught
8.4 million centners of fish, averaging 84.4 centners per fisherman. Wages per worker were 23.1 rubles per month in 1948
and 44.9 rubles per month in 1954.

From Sotsiologicheskie issledovaniia, 1975, no. 3, pp. 112-
21. The translation is by Michel Vale.

As our socialist economy grew stronger, the collective fisheries grew in strength as well. Beginning in 1954 (the second
stage) there occurred the first technical re-outfitting of the
fishing fleet. Small and medium-sized trawlers and seiners
appeared in the motorized fishing stations serving the collective fisheries. With their help the collective fisheries increased
their catch to 10 million centners. However, early in this stage
it was found that the more the basic means of production were
concentrated in the hands of the motorized fishing stations, the
less effectively they were used. It became clear that these
stations were not the answer to the question of raising the level
of development of collective fisheries. In accordance with the
resolution of the Central Committee of the Communist Party of
the Soviet Union and the Council of Ministers of the USSR of
February 9, 1959, all the basic means of production belonging
to these motorized fishing stations were placed directly in the
hands of the collective fisheries themselves. The collectives
were thereby transformed from renters of the basic means of
production into socialist productive collectives with their own
work force and their own means of production.

Thus began the third stage in the postwar development of
collective fisheries. This stage was characterized by a
strengthening of their material and technological base and
steady growth in their economy. In ten years the value of the
collectives' fleet increased fourfold, and there was a sixfold
increase in the total value of their basic means of production.
While from 1946 to 1960 the catch remained practically at the
same level, in the period from 1961 through 1970 it doubled.

Now that they had themselves become the controllers of the
basic means of production, the fishery workers considerably
improved all their productive and economic indices: productivity, the profitability of the fish industry, returns on investment, and wages increased. The increase in the productivity
of labor in the fishing industry outpaced the growth in wages,
which means that on the whole the collective fishing industry
improved its operations. A major factor in this development
was payment based on the final product of labor, a system that

historically had been used in collective fisheries from the very beginning, but whose incentive effect could not be realized fully until the basic means of production were in the hands of the collectives themselves. Accordingly, in the collective fisheries the workers are remunerated on the basis of the collective, aggregate final product of the socially necessary labor of the entire production collective. This system of payment for the final results of labor, as it is used in collective fisheries, has two organically interrelated aspects. First, there are rates per unit of output on the basis of which the wages of the collective participating in the production of this output are calculated. These rates are derived as a certain percentage deduction from the value of the total catch. The amount of these deductions is set at a general meeting of the collective fishery workers in accordance with the kind of catch and the degree of mechanization involved in fishing. It varies from 20% to 55% of the value of the fish delivered to the state. For example, the state purchase price for herring is 25 rubles per centner; the crew of RS-300 type seiners receives 5 rubles for each centner. The state purchase price of flounder is 18 rubles; the crew receives 4.5 rubles for each centner. Knowing the size of the deduction and the amount of fish delivered, each collective can easily determine what its remuneration would be per day, week, season, or for any period of time worked.

The other aspect of this pay system involved an assessment of the efforts contributed by each member of the collective to the total labor activity. Many years of practical experience and economic calculations have resulted in the establishment of a stable system of coefficients describing a worker's participation in overall labor activity: a system of shares. Analytic in its nature, this system provides in aggregate form a quite accurate assessment of the experience, level of training, skill, and importance of each worker in the total collective process of labor activity. The following shares have been established in actual practice for ship crews: seaman or fisherman first class — 1.0; boatsman — 1.2; radio operator — 1.2; trawlerman — 1.4; senior trawlerman — 1.6; mechanic's assistant —

1.5; senior captain's assistant — 1.7; senior mechanic — 1.9; ship captain — 2.0 shares.

Such a system of payment is simple and intelligible to each worker as well as being accessible to their control and supervision. This is its merit. In addition these norms remain in force for many years, i.e., they are solid and reliable; hence, when workers enter the labor process, they are fully confident that the grounds on which payment for their labor is determined will not change. Finally, the pay system in collective fisheries gives the worker unlimited perspectives (as far as external obstacles are concerned) for further increasing the productivity of labor and their remuneration, since any amount of fish caught and delivered, no matter how large the catch, will be accounted for and paid according to the same rates.

All these factors in production relations generate in the workers of collective fisheries a deep and firm interest in the maximum development of their social production and engender in them a high degree of satisfaction with the social relations within which their labor activity takes place.

Three Aspects of Work Satisfaction

Most collective fishery workers derive constant satisfaction from their labor. This important social result is in fact a general reflection of the productive and economic relations existing in collective fisheries. It is confirmed by objective data on the rapid development of collective production as well as the workers' assessment of their own work activity. Let us examine three important questions that clearly and directly support this conclusion.

To the survey question "Do you get satisfaction from your work?" workers in different areas of the country quite distant from one another gave almost identical responses. Most workers (over 73%) were satisfied with their work, one third were always satisfied, and two thirds experienced some periods of grievances but on the whole were also satisfied with their work.

The number of those who were completely dissatisfied was very small — about 4%. This is about half the natural turnover of the work force, which is usually accepted as 6-8%. Consequently, its explanation can be sought in various personal and incidental factors and circumstances deriving from the individual characteristics of particular workers. But clearly this group may also include people who are acutely sensitive to the negative aspects of collective fisheries. If we add them to people who are more frequently dissatisfied than satisfied with their work, we can conclude that almost every fifth worker in collective fisheries is looking for a qualitatively different kind of work than he is presently doing.

The concepts of "work" and "job" are very similar, but they do not completely coincide. The concept of "job" is more concrete, more closely linked to the specific features of the branch of production in which an individual's labor activity occurs. Hence, when a worker evaluates his job from the point of view of its content, attractiveness, and interest, he may either confirm his initial assessment of work satisfaction by introducing a new element, or he may cast doubt on the reliability of his initial assessment. A job that does not arouse interest usually does not make for work satisfaction. Hence answers to the question "How on the whole do you evaluate your job?" were regarded as control answers intended to support or cast doubt on answers to the first question. But at the same time, answers to the second question help shed light on a very important aspect of work satisfaction — the internal substantive aspect of this concept, which is not related to work in general but to the concrete type of work called a "job."

From answers to the second question it is evident that most workers liked their jobs. In any case, those who completely disliked their jobs were a negligible minority: 3.8%. This figure is similar to the figure for the number of workers experiencing only irritation from their work. Hence the same persons are reflected in these two figures. This supports our premise that people who do not like their jobs cannot experience complete satisfaction from their work, no matter how pleasant and favorable the situation in which it takes place.

The third question, which was designed to shed light on yet one more extremely important aspect of work satisfaction, had an even more concrete character: "How do you usually feel on the job?" The question has a direct bearing on the concept of "satisfaction." In addition, only answers to questions of this type can give a definitive assessment of work satisfaction. Indeed, if I am always satisfied with my work. I will usually experience satisfaction in the very process of work; if I am not satisfied, then in the process of work I will be full of negative feelings. We obtained the following answers in different areas of the industry (see Table 1).

From these findings it is evident that most workers of collective fisheries felt in a good and involved mood during the work process, and consequently the high degree of satisfaction that we referred to earlier not only showed up in their daily work routine but also derived directly from the productive process. Over one fourth of all workers worked calmly and with concentration, since the work process itself interested them. On the whole, more than half were in a good and involved mood during work. Thus about 80% of workers of collective fisheries experience satisfaction not only in general and on the whole, in the light of the results of their labor, but also in the process of work itself. This is of fundamental importance, since only when the work process itself brings with it a good mood, satisfaction, and joy is the eternal contradiction between work and life removed: work is then regarded not as a "sacrifice" but as life itself. From the data presented here it is evident that work satisfaction is a product of a strengthening unity between the process of labor and its results.

Some Social Factors Determining the Attitude toward Work

What are the factors responsible for the high level of work satisfaction of workers under the production and economic relationships existing in collective fisheries" Since under social-

Table 1

Responses	Far East	North Sea	Baltic	Black Sea and Sea of Azov	Caspian	Average for collective
1. I always work calmly and with concentration since the work interests me	22.0	26.0	26.0	29.0	27.1	26.0
2. Sometimes I feel agitated and irritated, but on the whole I am in a good and involved mood during work	57.4	56.1	50.0	46.0	53.3	52.6
3. I always feel agitated and irritated due to the poor organization of work	13.3	10.7	15.0	17.0	14.0	14.0
4. I am frequently nervous and argue with others and have many unpleasant moments	6.0	4.9	4.1	5.4	4.1	4.9
5. No response	1.3	2.3	4.9	2.6	1.4	2.5
Total	100	100	100	100	100	100

ism labor is primarily a means of existence, satisfaction with one's work should derive mainly from the high wages received in collective fisheries. If this is the case, there should be a direct proportional relationship between wages and work satisfaction, i.e., the higher the wages, the higher should be the degree of satisfaction.

However, our analysis (see Table 2) did not show a direct

relationship between the wage level and attitudes toward work; although the wages of fishermen vary quite considerably from one region of the country to another, variations in attitude toward work are more local and intraregional in character. Consequently, it is not just the level of wages but other factors as well that influence work attitudes. But what are these factors?

Table 2

Regions	Average monthly earnings of fishermen in 1969	Always or frequently satisfied with work	Consider their jobs interesting, like their jobs	Always in a good mood during work
		% surveyed		
Astrakhan Region	138	43.4	37.2	55.8
Leningrad Region	181	57.8	65.8	68.4
Estonian SSR	211	74.7	59.6	82.2
Arkhangelsk Region	233	51.3	34.9	74.3
Murmansk Region	224	58.8	44.7	73.0
Latvian SSR	233	57.1	48.4	66.2
Kaliningrad Region	261	60.0	56.2	74.7
Lithuania SSR	320	50.9	52.6	72.0
Kamchatka Region	404	58.8	41.0	69.4
Khabarovsk Territory	410	57.5	50.0	62.9
Sakhalin Region	444	63.1	52.5	72.1

Let us analyze the mechanism through which the material incentives determining workers' attitudes toward their work operate, i.e., the particular system of payment. In the collective fisheries we studied, a fisherman's remuneration for labor was directly proportional to its final results: the larger the catch, the higher the pay.

An important peculiarity of the pay system in this branch is the principle of the proportional participation in the final results of labor, or the share system, as it is called, which enables each worker to determine his share of remuneration with an accuracy down to the nearest ruble. Our studies showed a connection between work satisfaction and attitudes toward this system of shares as the chief instrument of payment to fishermen (see Table 3).

Table 3

Are you satisfied with your work?	Size of share corresponds to labor expended	Size of share does not correspond to labor expended
Yes, always	80.4	19.6
Every now and then I am disappointed, but on the whole I feel satisfied with my work	76.0	24.0
I am more often dissatisfied than satisfied	59.1	41.9
I am never satisfied and feel only irritation and displeasure	51.6	48.4

Whether the attitude toward work was positive or negative, the connection between work satisfaction and the specific mechanism of payment was obvious. As satisfaction decreases, confidence in the fairness of the share system also decreases. But even among those who are continuously dissatisfied with their work, more than half consider the share system fair, namely, that it justly determines their contribution to the joint labor process. Obviously, a sense of fairness makes for a positive attitude toward work. The fact that almost 20% of the workers who were satisfied with their work did not consider that the share system gave a fully adequate assessment of their real contribution to production does not at all contradict this conclusion. Dissatisfaction with work is also connected with the pay system, but this is a more complex relationship. The attitude toward work of those who considered the pay system fair, yet nevertheless were dissatisfied with their work, was influenced by other factors having nothing to do with the pay system.

To check this assertion, let us examine the relationship between the fishermens' assessment of their respective shares and their evaluation of their jobs (see Table 4).

Table 4

How on the whole do you evaluate your job?	Size of share corresponds to labor expended	Size of share does not correspond to labor expended
Job is interesting; I like it	73.1	29.6
Job is no worse and no better than any other	73.6	27.4
Job is not interesting; I do not like it	55.8	44.2

The table bears out the conclusions we have already drawn: a correspondence between payment and amount of work performed, i.e., the perception of payment as fair or unfair was, indeed, a factor determining attitude toward work. Payment based on the final results of labor was valued very highly by the collective fishery workers, and even those who were not satisfied with their work in most cases regarded this system positively. However, these are not the only factors: they op-

erate together with other social and economic factors that had
to be ascertained.

Because of the social nature of labor, individual efforts are
fused together with the aggregate work effort of the collective
to which the individual belongs. Hence an extremely important
social and economic factor determining a worker's attitude toward work is his participation in the management of the productive process in which his work collective is engaged.

Let us compare the attitudes of members of a work collective
toward their jobs with their direct participation in the discussion of methods and means of performing their jobs.

The data in Table 5 show that job attitude and participation
in the management of the actual labor process are interrelated.
Workers who take part in such management feel that their jobs
are interesting. Conversely, those who feel their jobs are not
interesting do not take part in management. Interest in one's
job decreases as active participation in management decreases.
The index of contrast confirms this: for those who like their
jobs, the difference between those who participate in management and those who do not is +49.1, while for those who dislike
their jobs this index is −4.5. However, these data also indicate
that this relationship is a complex one, that there are other factors
involved that have a marked influence on people's behavior.

In production it is not only the material elements of production that are managed but also the workers involved in a particular production process. We attempted to relate this factor
to workers' satisfaction with their jobs (Table 6).

The table shows a clear relationship between job attitudes and
workers' participation in dealing with questions bearing on peo-
ples' behavior. When work attitudes were positive, the relationship was directly proportional; when they were negative, the relationship was inversely proportional. However, in this case
the indices were much lower in absolute terms than the indices
characterizing participation in the management of production.
Indeed, whereas most workers were involved in deciding questions bearing purely on production (through meetings, conferences, instruction sessions, collective proposals and the opin-

Table 5

How on the whole do you evaluate your job?	Do you take part in dis- cussions on methods and techniques to be used in your job?			Index of contrast
	yes	seldom	no	
Job is interesting; I like it	66.7	15.7	17.6	+49.1
Job is no worse and no better than any other	47.3	20.3	32.4	+14.9
Job is not interesting; I do not like it	37.3	20.9	41.8	−4.5

Table 6

How on the whole do you evaluate your job?	Do you take part in discussing ques- tions about the behavior, rewards, and punishment of your comrades in the work collective?			index
	yes	seldom	no	
Job is interesting; I like it	52.3	15.5	32.3	+20.0
Job is no worse and no better than any other	33.0	21.0	41.0	−3.0
Job is not interesting; I do not like it	30.0	22.0	48.0	−18.0

ions of members of the group), very often only a limited number of workers, and at times only the "triumvirate," participated in decisions having to do with rewarding or punishing people.

Finally, let us examine the relationship between job attitudes and the participation of workers in deciding questions having to do with the partial distribution of the results of production, with the distribution and awarding of various premiums accruing to the collective (Table 7).

Table 7

How on the whole do you evaluate your job?	Do you take part in the distribution of premiums awarded to your collective?			
	yes	seldom	no	index
Job is interesting; I like it	31.2	10.5	58.3	− 27.1
Job is no worse and no better than any other	30.0	11.1	58.9	− 28.9
Job is not interesting; I do not like it	25.4	3.6	71.0	− 45.6

In this case we also find a direct relationship between positive and negative attitudes toward work on the one hand, and workers' participation in the distribution of bonuses on the other. A sharp decrease in the indices reflecting participation in the distribution of premium points to a low degree of participation of workers in the distribution of the results of their labor. Whereas the index was +49.1 for those who participated in management of the production process and who liked their jobs, it fell to − 27.1 for those who participated in the distribution of premiums and who liked their jobs. Evi-

dently, a certain number of workers who have a positive attitude toward their jobs were kept from participating in decisions
on very important questions bearing on the social life of their
work collectives.

A study of all the questions bearing on the participation of
workers in the management of various aspects of the collective's life goes beyond the bounds of this study. Nonetheless,
we did ask collective fishery workers one general question having to do with a sense of "being their own boss" and in general
reflecting the degree of their participation in the management
of the affairs of their cooperative (Table 8).

Table 8

Attitude toward job	Do you feel you are your own boss in your collective?				
	yes		no		index
I always get satisfaction from work	307	71.7	121	28.3	+43.4
Frequently	726	43.8	546	56.2	+12.4
I more often do not get satisfaction	76	22.1	267	77.9	−55.8
I am constantly dissatisfied with work	17	20.7	65	79.3	−58.6
Job is interesting; I like it	652	57.0	492	43.0	+14.0
Job is no better and no worse than any other	253	33.3	505	66.7	−33.4
Job is not interesting; I do not like it	16	20.0	64	80.0	−60.0
I always work calmly and with concentration	357	65.9	156	30.1	+39.8
I am in a positive and busy mood	479	43.5	621	56.5	−13.0
I experience annoyance on the job	57	23.2	188	76.8	−53.6
I am always nervous	18	22.2	63	77.8	−55.6

A comparison of the answers to this question with data on work satisfaction, job assessment, and how people felt in the labor process showed that participation in managing the affairs of the collective was one of the social factors that had a significant effect on the shaping of workers' attitudes toward their labor activity. Table 8 supports the findings shown in all the other tables and at the same time clearly reveals the degree of contrast in the distribution of answers depending on whether work attitudes were positive or negative. The range of variation in the index reaches almost 100 points. This indicates a sharp polarization in the worker's behavior depending on whether he is included in the process of managing the life of the collective.

Thus we can say that after the system of payment, the next most important social factor shaping a person's attitude toward work is his participation in the management of the life of the production collective of which he is a member.

Relative Significance of the Main Social Factors Determining Attitudes toward Work

Which of the factors shaping attitude toward work are of primary importance and which are of secondary importance, i.e., what is the significance of the major social factors determining work attitudes, both in terms of the influence of the individual factors on this attitude and of their influence relative to each other?

Using the method of latent analysis, we obtained the results shown in Table 9. In first place with regard to significance among other factors and the degree of influence exerted on job attitude is general participation in conducting the affairs of the collective. This result agrees with the socioeconomic nature of cooperative collectives as voluntary associations of people coming together for joint collective labor on the basis of common possession of cooperative means of production. Participation in management is of decisive importance for the shaping of an optimally positive attitude toward work activity among

members of the collective. However, this participation is still
inadequate in actual practice, and the skillful utilization of this
factor is an important source for raising labor productivity and
increasing social production. To be specific, the role of rank-
and-file members of collective fisheries and other production
collectives in deciding fundamental questions must be increased.
This conclusion is in full accordance with the need for further
intensification and stricter observance of the basic principles
of economic accounting in all branches of collective production
as the chief economic mechanism for managing the economy
and as the basic economic form for managing labor activity,
stimulating initiative, and fostering the creativity of collectives
directly engaged in production; the feasibility of such a system
is premised on a highly developed and functioning democracy
within the collective units.

General participation in conducting the collective's affairs
consists of two important factors for both the individual worker
and the work collective: first, management of the process of
production itself, during the course of which the individual
worker is both the organizer and executor of his work; second,
management of the distribution of the results of this production
by means of a system of material remuneration that provides
the most objective and fair equivalence between the measure
of individual-collective labor and the measure of its material
remuneration. Both these factors are organically interrelated.
Without an intelligent and skillful management of the productive process, there will be no large returns to distribute. And
without correct distribution it is impossible to intelligently
manage the production process and to achieve good results.
Hence our scale of degrees of significance places these factors
a whole order of magnitude (14 points) lower than the principal
factor that combines them, namely, "a sense of being one's
own boss"; but they are very similar to one another, differing
by only 3 points (0.23 and 0.20), which underlines the vitally
important role of these factors in actual practice.

Our scale of degrees of significance shows that participation
of the workers in the management of the production process is

Table 9

Scale of Degrees of Significance of Social
Factors Determining Job Attitudes

Main factor	Job is interesting; I like it — index	Job is no worse and no better than any other — index	Scale
General participation in managing affairs of collective (feels "I am my own boss")	+0.11	−0.26	0.37
System of payment as a mechanism for coordinating measure of work expended and measure of remuneration	+0.17	−0.03	0.20
Participation in managing production process	+0.33	+0.10	0.23
Participation in social life of collective	+0.12	−0.20	0.14
Participation in distribution of privileges and bonuses	−0.15	−0.28	0.13
Specific system of shares in general system of payment	+0.20	+0.15	0.05

considerably higher than their participation in determining the
remuneration that should be given in accordance with work.
Participation in the management of the production process for
those who found their jobs interesting had an index of +0.33,
while those whose job attitudes were just average had an index
of +0.10. However, participation in determining the share of
remuneration among those who found their jobs interesting had
an index that was only half as high (+0.17), while for those
whose job attitudes were average, the index was negative
(−0.03), i.e., the situation was clearly unsatisfactory for this
category of workers. This is why an increase in the role of
workers in determining how much should be paid for work performed by each participant in the collective process of production is an urgent problem, which, if it is resolved satisfactorily,
will have a strong influence on increasing labor productivity
and raising the efficiency of collective production.

The next two social factors helping to determine job attitudes
have an importance that is a whole order lower (6 points) than
the preceding ones, although again they are quite close to one
another. Participation in the social life of the production collective has a scale index of 0.14, while participation in the
distribution of supplementary kinds of material incentives has
an index of 0.13. Consequently, these factors are very similar
in their potential impact on shaping positive work attitudes.

In actual practice these factors, especially the second, are
by no means always adequately utilized. Workers are often
not very actively involved in distributing supplementary kinds
of material rewards in accordance with annual results or when
seasonal work is completed. This reduces their active participation in the labor process and inhibits the development of
a sense of being full collective controllers of the means of production.

We should underscore the significance of the factor of participation in dealing with questions of the behavior, rewards,
and punishment of one's comrades in joint work activity. For
those who found their job interesting, this factor had a positive
index (+0.12), which indicates that they played an active role

in dealing with these questions. For those who found their jobs of average interest, this index was negative (− 0.02), indicating that these persons were somewhat removed from deciding problems concerning the behavior of their comrades, and hence pointing to the need for more complete utilization of democratic forms of managing the life of production collectives.

A specific system of shares can be an important element in the system of payment and hence can exert a considerable influence on people's attitudes toward their jobs and toward work in general. Our scale of degrees of significance of the major factors shows that this factor has a positive index (+0.20 and +0.15), which confirms the satisfactory attitude of fishermen toward this extremely important element relating to distribution and the determination of the amount of individual remuneration. It had the lowest value on the scale, 0.05, standing below other factors that should be utilized to a degree commensurate with their importance in shaping optimal job attitudes among workers of collective fisheries.

Note

1. This article is based on the results of a comprehensive social and economic study conducted in collective fisheries between 1969 and 1971, under the direction of the author, by researchers of the Plekhanov Institute of Economics. The survey covered 2,942 members of these collectives, including 2,016 fishermen.

THE INFLUENCE OF A WORKER'S ON-THE-JOB INDEPENDENCE ON HIS ATTITUDE TOWARD WORK

A. V. Tikhonov

Many empirical studies in the sociology of labor today take as their theoretical point of departure a certain conceptual framework that presents in compact form a variety of factors and indices bearing on the attitude toward work and the main relationships among them.[1] There can be no doubt that this framework has had a positive impact on raising the theoretical level of research. Indeed, it is important in the sense that in this framework, for the first time, Marxist methodology is applied in integral form to the area of empirical research into the shaping of attitudes toward work, with attention focused on the objective, specific conditions of labor activity (the various elements in the production situation) and on how they are refracted in the individuals' motivations. Another achievement of this conceptual framework has been to formulate the question of the leading role played by so specific a factor as the content of a job in the shaping of an individual's attitude toward work, since without progress in the material conditions of labor and the associated enhancement of the creative potential offered

Russian text © 1976 by "Nauka" Publishers. From Sotsio-logicheskie issledovaniia, 1976, no. 1, pp. 31-44. Translated by Michel Vale.

by work, it would be difficult to speak seriously about the development of the individual and the transformation of labor into a primary need of life.

More recent studies have focused on specific aspects of the problem of work initiative, work satisfaction, etc. "Competing factors" emerged — from working conditions and the socio-demographic characteristics of workers, to various social and sociopsychological characteristics of work collectives. A mass of factual data was gathered. However, the further subdivision of the area of research into particular topics entails certain dangers. It has required the continued refinement and development of the conceptual framework as a whole, particularly since it had first been formulated before a good deal of important theoretical and methodological research in the labor area had been conducted.[2]

In the present article we attempt to formulate more precisely the concept of a leading specific factor in work attitudes and the structure of indices reflecting these attitudes. We shall be studying the mutual influence of such factors as the functional content of work and on-the-job independence, i.e., the independence of the worker in the productive process, on attitudes toward work. Indices of work attitudes are presented as indices reflecting the labor process and its results. The conceptual potential of this approach has been tested in empirical studies, the results of which are examined in the following.

Methods and Procedures

The main purpose of the study was to investigate the influence of the following factors on the objective characteristics of labor activity: (a) the main trends in technical progress and related changes in the functional content of work, and (b) the main ways to improve the socialist social organization of production (referred to as production organization below) and, in particular, changes in the structure of workers' functions in managing their own labor process. We have chosen the expres-

sion "on-the-job independence" to refer to these functions and
to reflect the investment of workers with the social functions
of control and management of the labor process by the production organization, in contrast to a "technological" independence,
which reflects the degree of freedom that the individual enjoys
by virtue of technology and production techniques.

Recent literature reflects a one-sided interpretation of the
problem of improving the content of work. The main stress is
placed on the enrichment of work by the gradual transfer of
energy functions and certain other functions from the individual
to the machine. This process is reflected empirically in the
increasing role of intellectual functions performed by workers
on the job (something that has been clearly established in a
number of studies) and in the increasing proportion of workers
possessing a broad range of competence in repair and align-
ment and operating skills in the occupational structure.[3] Thus
enrichment in the content of work is seen as proceeding only
along a horizontal dimension, i.e., as a result of the redistribution of functions within the "man—machine" system. But the
vertical component, namely, the distribution of functions between work involving the actual performance and carrying out
of operations, on the one hand, and work concerned with control and management, on the other, has been ignored. However,
the creative opportunities of a job are determined not only by
what must be done but also by how it is to be done. The limits
of this "how" are in large measure defined by the relationship
between performance functions and control and management
functions, or in our terminology, by the level of a worker's
on-the-job independence.

Neglect of this factor, i.e., a worker's on-the-job independence, has impoverished the conceptual framework of research
and has impeded progress in dealing with the problem of attitudes toward work at both the theoretical and applied levels.
At the theoretical level an important social factor, whose ori-
gins go back to the epoch in which manufacturing production
first appeared, is lost sight of. For it was during this period
that the integral structure of the work performed by the free

craftsman became fragmented, and he was transformed into an "appendage of a particular machine."[4] <u>What</u> to do and <u>how</u> to do it were henceforth predetermined by the capitalist mode of production. Under socialism the social and economic obstacles to the transformation of previously fragmented labor into an integral activity of freely associated workers are removed. However, there still remains a certain amount of "nonfreedom" in the technical and social organization of work that will only be overcome as socialist labor is transformed into communist labor.

Today this process is being furthered at many levels by major efforts to improve the effective participation of workers in the management of production. However, it must be borne in mind that participation in management through voluntary activity in social organizations [na obshchestvennykh nachalakh] amounts to no more than compensation for the social costs of strictly regulated work involving routine execution of directives. However an integral personality is shaped only on the basis of an integral activity in which the functions of performing work and managing work are combined in the labor process of the direct producer.

In practical terms the issue concerns the problems of the social organization of socialist production as new techniques and progressive technology are introduced and as management systems are improved (in particular, the introduction of systems for the automatic control of production, the elimination of multilevel structures, reaping the advantages of the socialist division of labor and socialist cooperation). As enterprises and economic associations approach the stage of comprehensive automation of production and the use of personnel with new types of skills, the problem of on-the-job independence assumes a more acute form. What degree of independence of workers in the planning, organization, and control and management of their own work should be considered optimal from the social and economic point of view? How should the system of long-range and day-to-day decision-making be restructured at the different levels of management? At the present time it is dif-

ficult to find any well-grounded answers to these questions. It
is generally thought that planning of the structure and functions
of management from an economic perspective will automatically
also solve social problems, including the question of the opti-
mum level of on-the-job independence. The practical upshot of
this is that the coordination between "technological" and "on-
the-job" independence takes place spontaneously and blindly,
and hence by no means always on optimal terms; and this, we
think, has an effect on the principal characteristics of work
attitudes.

In our opinion the structure of indices bearing on work attitudes should reflect as closely as possible the structure of real
work activity. It would be a vast oversimplification to say that
the so-called objective indices of work attitudes (productivity,
quality of work, conscientiousness, discipline, initiative, etc.)
are all factors of the same order that can be arbitrarily dis-
aggregated or combined at will. We know from practical experience in industry that a one-sided emphasis on the achievement of high quantitative results is often accompanied by a decrease in the quality of work, while efforts to strengthen on-
the-job discipline may reduce initiative. The relationships
among these indices are not up to the whims of the investigator
but are the result of the operation of various mechanisms of
labor management that have evolved in a particular enterprise.
It is a reasonable requirement that a study of work attitudes
in terms of objective indices should be directed toward ascer-
taining the acutal discontinuities in the structure of these indices. The division of indices of work attitudes into objective
and subjective is only one possible division that chiefly stresses
the relationship between motivation and behavior. At the same
time, it shifts the problem of work attitudes to another level,
the sociological and psychological.[5]

But it is no less important to study the structure of labor activity itself, and in this Marx's definition of labor as a purpose-
ful activity applying the instruments of labor to the object of
labor to obtain significant results can serve as a methodological key. He wrote: "In the process of labor human activity uses

the instruments of labor to bring about a prefigured change in the object of labor. The process is consumated in the product."[6] Marx distinguishes here at least two basic structures, constituting the process of labor or labor itself and its results (products). In the labor process the individual enters into relations with other participants in production in the course of utilizing the instruments of labor, while in the results of labor, relations are constituted on the basis of an assessment of the social value of the product, which is part of the process of distribution of goods. The evolution of an attitude toward work as a prime vital need may be interpreted as a gradual shift in the assessment of the social value of labor from the result (product) to the process of labor itself. In this sense the distinction between indices referring to the labor process and those concerning the results of labor in a worker's activity may be of definite interest in clarifying the problem of concern here.

Our study distinguished two groups of basic variables (see the chart on p. 106), which on the one hand represented the functional content of labor and the workers' on-the-job independence and, on the other, indices of work attitudes related to the labor process and its results.

The theoretical assumption on which our study was based was that the problem of work attitudes can be studied as a problem of the shift in the purpose of labor from the result to the process of labor, as the degree to which the "leading specific factors," namely, the functional content of work and the on-the-job independence of the worker, are brought increasingly closer together. It was not our purpose, of course, to provide a complete empirical verification of this hypothesis.

Three corollary hypotheses were specifically tested. (1) The objective indices of a worker's labor activity, recorded during the course of an investigation within the framework of a specific organization of production, have a complex structure marked by a discrepancy between the indices relating to the labor process and those relating to the results of labor. It was expected that a correlation analysis of the connections between the particular indices would reveal stable groups.

A. V. Tikhonov

Pattern of Basic Variables in the Study

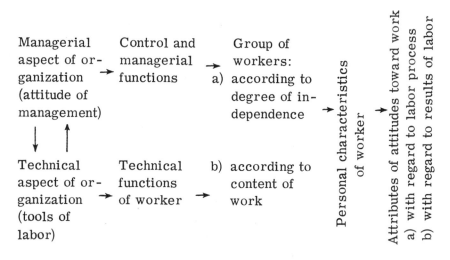

(2) The functional content of labor and a worker's on-the-job independence are determined by different factors; as a result, they are relatively independent of one another, and on-the-job independence can be dealt with separately as a significant object of enquiry in its own right. In testing this hypothesis, we expected that we would find either an increase (or a decrease) in the degree of on-the-job independence as we moved from one group of workers (defined in terms of job content) to another (which would be a refutation of the hypothesis) or a lack of any significant correlation (which would confirm the hypothesis). (3) Finally, the on-the-job independence of a worker has just as strong an influence on indices reflecting work attitudes as the content of job functions; this hypothesis stresses the complex nature of the determinants of labor activity. We proposed to determine the relationships between these factors and the indices of the labor process and of the results of labor.

To some extent we repeated the well-known studies of work attitudes among the young workers of Leningrad. At the same time, in accordance with our present purposes, we studied the distribution of control and managerial functions among workers on jobs having different functional contents and formulated more precisely the structure of objective indices of work attitudes.

The novelty in our study consisted in how we defined the object of our enquiry. We assumed that general social factors are not simply refracted through the prism of the functional content of work but affect the structure of the personality as well. Above all they determine the particular type of local production organization in which work content, personality, and work attitudes are functionally related to the goals of the production organization and the means used to achieve them.

Based on these considerations, we undertook a study of the entire work force of a single enterprise. It was especially desirable that the enterprise should have a highly dynamic technical foundation, have attained the level of comprehensive automation of production, use technically advanced and technically backward production processes at the same time, and enjoy a considerable degree of organizational autonomy.

All these requirements were met by the "Al'met'evskneft'" oil-extracting enterprise, which is part of the "Tatneft'" industrial association. At the time the main survey was taken, the enterprise had about 3,500 workers.[7] It was responsible for 7-8% of the total petroleum production in the Soviet Union, which gives some idea of the large scale of its production.

To test our hypotheses, we distinguished various groups of workers according to increasing functional content of work, degree of on-the-job independence, and attitude toward work.

The grouping according to work content was based on such criteria as level of mechanization, the set of technical functions involved in servicing technological processes (supervision, management, supplementing of machine work with manual work, purely manual work, adjustment, maintenance and repair work), and the relative amount of intellectual and physical energy required.[8] In addition, we took into account the position of a given occupation within the functional structure of production (basic, auxiliary, servicing). The following groups were thus distinguished: (1) highly skilled manual labor in adjusting, repair,

and maintenance of technological equipment in partially automated and mechanized production; (2) highly skilled work in
the management and control of technological processes in highly
mechanized production; (3) skilled work in the management and
control of technological processes in partially automated and
highly mechanized production; (4) skilled work using machinery
and mechanical devices in mechanized production; (5) skilled
work of the craftsman type; (6) skilled work of the subsidiary
type involving attending a technological process in mechanized
production; (7) low-skilled auxiliary work in mechanized production; (8) low-skilled manual labor of the manufacturing type;
(9) unskilled labor.

The level of on-the-job independence was defined as the degree to which control, recordkeeping, and managerial functions
were present in a worker's job. The managerial function was
defined according to the following criteria: (1) planning of the
worker's task; (2) organization of the performance of the job in
terms of supervision and recordkeeping with respect to (a) the degree of supervision over the performance of the job, and (b)
the "rigor" with which job performance is recorded.[9]

To keep our indices free from distortions introduced by the
subjective attitudes of managers and subordinates, and by their
personal qualities, the occupation itself was selected as the
bearer of information, just as in the measurement of the functional content of work. An occupation that received the highest
number of points with respect to the indicated criteria was
given the highest rating for on-the-job independence. We thus
distinguished seven groups of occupations ranked according to
the degree of on-the-job independence from very high to very
low.

The main objective indices of work attitude were: productivity, quality of work, participation in rationalization, initiative in achieving results (these were the indices of the results
of labor); thoroughness with which technological functions were
performed, concern for the use of the instruments of labor
(machinery, mechanical devices, instruments), concern for the
use of materials and work time, helping in the labor process

(these were the indices of the labor process itself). We also used an auxiliary list of indices[10] that generally enabled us to distribute workers first according to indices of the results of labor and then according to the labor process itself.

The following were distinguished in the first type of division: (1) highly skilled workers who actively tried to improve efficiency, systematically overfulfilled their production targets, and always did work of high quality; (2) workers who overfulfilled production targets, whose work was always of good quality, and whose initiative was average; (3) workers who fulfilled production targets, did work of average quality, and showed an average level of initiative; (4) workers who fulfilled production targets erratically, did work of below-average quality, and showed poor initiative; (5) workers who did not fulfill production targets, did work of poor quality, and showed no initiative. In terms of the second criterion, we distinguished the following groups: (1) workers who were very meticulous in carrying out technical functions, showed considerable concern in their use of techniques, instruments, materials, and work time, and always helped their comrades on the job; (2) workers who fulfilled technical functions, tried to make better use of their technical tools, materials, and time, and who helped their comrades on the job; (3) workers whose fulfillment of technical functions was somewhat unsatisfactory, who made average use of the potential offered by machinery and mechanical devices, who were somewhat wasteful of time and materials, and who showed an average readiness to help others; (4) workers who fulfilled only the basic technical functions, who showed no effort to save time and materials, and who were somewhat negligent about helping others; (5) workers whose fulfillment of technical functions was quite unsatisfactory, who made poor use of the tools of labor, and who wasted a considerable amount of time and materials.

The procedure and techniques of the study were determined by the problems we set for ourselves. Information about the main tendencies for change in the technical characteristics of the enterprise and its organizational structure was obtained by studying documentary sources (performance reports from 1962 and materials from the technical, industrial, and financial plan of 1971-75 were used). To determine work content for the different occupations, we examined 960 photographs recording the workday and analyzed workers' own accounts of their jobs. In addition, we made use of assessments of possible changes in job content of occupations for the period 1971-75 given by shop and department superintendents in formal interviews.

First, information necessary to determine the level of on-the-job independence of workers was obtained from the record cards of interviews of shop supervisors and workers. Then, from the ratings thus obtained we computed average indices for each occupation. These indices were further refined in conjunction with the enterprise management. Here we tried to reflect as accurately as possible the actually existing regulation of job performance with regard to planning, organization of execution, and control of the work.

Our study of the functional content of jobs and the degree of workers' independence covered all the occupations represented in the enterprise — 71 occupations (3,448 workers). Occupational titles were derived from the most recent job and pay handbook for the petroleum-extracting industry (1970).

Information regarding work attitudes was obtained from workers' record cards filled out in the course of interviews with foremen. Some of the information was checked against the enterprise's files. The data agreed well. The sample was selected according to occupational groups and checked in terms of social and demographic characteristics. Work attitudes were assessed twice, with a six-month interval. The first time the ratings were anonymous (and included 1,360 workers); the second time they were with names (1,600 workers). The information collected was tested and found to be statistically reliable. In this article we will be using material from the second survey. The persons doing the evaluation were 106 shop foremen and section heads.

In processing the accumulated data, the ranking of occupations according to various criteria played an important role.

These criteria were the functional content of the job, the degree
of on-the-job independence of the workers, and work attitudes.
Indices based on a weighted, mean point rating were used to
obtain summary evaluations of occupations with regard to the
parameter of on-the-job independence. The significance of the
various characteristics of work attitudes were calculated for
each occupation (index i). The procedure used to calculate the
index was the one proposed in the study Man and His Work
[Chelovek i ego rabota], albeit with certain modifications.[11]
The index reflecting the significance of a particular characteristic of work attitude was calculated according to the following
formula for each group of workers:

$$i = \frac{nk}{N},$$

where N is the number of workers in the given occupation, k
is the number of values for the characteristic, and n is the
frequency of distribution of workers according to the values
of the given characteristic.

The sense of the index is as a qualitative expression of the
relationship between the theoretical and actual frequency of
the distribution of workers according to each characteristic
(between $\frac{N}{k}$ and n). The value of the characteristic having
the highest index was considered the modal one. Since an increase in the value of the characteristic in excess of the modal
value reflected a positive characteristic of work attitude, the
corresponding i values were given a plus sign, while values
below the modal value were given a minus sign.

The modal sign itself was considered positive. The bound-
aries within which the values of the indices for all occupations
were situated were determined on the basis of the magnitude
of the index and its sign. Then we aggregated the indices for
occupations by groups (defined in terms of work content and
on-the-job independence) and calculated the mean indices relating to the process of labor and the results of labor.

The relationship between the ranked groups of occupations
was determined on the basis of a calculation of the Kendall and
Spearman coefficients.

The Main Results of the Study

The first hypothesis was tested by several methods. Even
a simple comparison of the frequency distributions of workers
according to the indices of the process of labor and the results
of labor reveals substantial divergences between these indices
(see Table 1).

Table 1

Attitude toward result of labor		Attitude toward process of labor	
group of workers	%	group of workers	%
1	4.0	1	4.5
2	27.3	2	37.2
3	47.5	3	38.4
4	16.8	4	15.4
5	4.4	5	4.5

Thus whereas the group of workers not carrying out technical functions with the required thoroughness, wasting work
time, etc., was the modal one with respect to the process of
labor, the group of workers fulfilling production tasks with an
average level of work quality and initiative was the modal one
with respect to the results of labor. If we regard fulfillment
and overfulfillment of production tasks with an output of definite quality as "normal," on the one hand, and complete fulfillment of technical functions, concern over techniques, materials, and the rational use of free time as "normal," on the other,
then 78.8% of the workers (groups 1-3) had high indices with
respect to the results of labor, while 41.7% (groups 1 and 2)

had high indices with respect to the process of labor, i.e., the difference between the two indices was on the order of 2 to 1.

Given the conditions at the enterprise where we carried out our study, inattentiveness to equipment in the course of carrying out production tasks may be explained by weaknesses in the setting of technical standards, the extensive use of a time-rate bonus system of payment, etc. However, a deeper explanation would consider the objective of the management of labor. The discrepancy between the indices for the process of labor and the result of labor stems from the predominant orientation of the production organization toward production goals, which shows up especially sharply in the stress placed on the quantitative results of labor.

The derivation of an intercorrelation matrix for 12 indices by the cluster method showed that initially the investigated characteristics functioned as an organic whole, and then, as the requirements placed on the strength of relationships became more rigorous, at a certain point they began to separate into several stable groups. The indices that were most weakly correlated with other indices were technical creativity (first cluster), discipline and observance of safety measures (second cluster), and labor productivity (third independent cluster). The quality of work was separated from the performance of production tasks and formed the most closely related independent cluster with the index of conscientiousness (sixth cluster). The fifth cluster was formed by indices of work attitudes related to the process of labor. A negative verification of these findings with regard to the strength of the internal and external relations of a group of characteristics (the β-coefficient method) confirmed the presence of stable clusters, including differences between indices bearing on the process of labor and the results of labor.[12]   On the whole, our first hypothesis was confirmed; at the same time, we noted the existence of a rather complex structure of relationships between the objective indices of work attitudes. This focuses our attention on this structure as an important subject of inquiry in its own right and compels us to be cautious about aggregating indices in an arbitrary way.

The second hypothesis was checked by assessing the level of
on-the-job independence of occupational groups distinguished
according to criteria of the functional content of work (see
Table 2).

The first column (ordinal numberals) ranks occupational
groups according to the functional content of work; the last column shows the level of independence of workers in the particular occupational group in terms of a weighted mean point rating.[13] Even a cursory glance at the relationship between the
point rating of on-the-job independence and the rank of the
group according to the functional content of work indicates the
lack of any clear connection between these factors. Indeed, our
calculation of Kendall's coefficient of rank correlation shows
0.08 (Spearman's is 0.112). A careful examination of the occupational groups shows that they were quite heterogeneous with
regard to on-the-job independence. Thus workers in the first
rank group (highly skilled manual labor in the repair, maintenance, and adjustment of technological equipment in partially
automated production) fell into two subgroups: those with an
average level of independence (machinists in ongoing maintenance and major repair of technological equipment, KIPiA fitters and maintenance electricians — 224 in all), and those with
a low level of independence (electricians on equipment maintenance and machinists — 403 persons). These subgroups also
differed in the type of independence. The work of the first
group was marked by "rigorously" assigned tasks (every day
or several times per day), a certain degree of independence
in performing the job (the workers themselves organized their
work place), little external supervision, and a measure of self-
accountability. In the second group, however, tighter supervision was combined with a rather average degree of self-
organization in receiving and executing job assignments. A
similar heterogenity was observed in all occupational groups.
The only exception was the ninth group. In this group the functions of unskilled manual labor of the manufacturing type were
combined with a low level of independence (this group included

Table 2

The Structure of Workers' Positions in the Production Organization
of a Petroleum-Extracting Enterprise*

Number and rank of occupational group*	Content of worker's position		Occupations	Number of workers	Average weighted point ratings of independence for occupational group
	functional content of work	independence of worker (presence of controlling, supervising, and managerial functions)			
1	Function of highly skilled manual labor in adjustment and maintenance of technological equipment in partially automated production	1. Average level of independence with preponderance of control functions	a) Day-to-day and major maintenance and repair men for technological equipment, KIP fitter	224	2.43
			b) Electrician, maintenance electrician for equipment, maintenance man	403	
2	Function of highly skilled labor in controlling and managing technological processes in comprehensive mechanized production	1. High level of independence with a balanced proportion a control and managerial functions	c) Petroleum processing operator	47	3.28
		2. Average level of independence with preponderance of managerial functions	d) KNS machinist, well investigating operator	141	

116

Group	Subcategory	Occupation	Number
8 Functions of low-skilled manual labor	3. Low level of self-organization with preponderance of managerial functions	e) KRS driller	12
	1. High level of independence with preponderance of managerial functions	f) Vulcanizer, carpenter, instrument maker, batcher, book binder, laboratory assistant, gas fitter, upholsterer, outfitter	163
	2. Average level of independence with preponderance of managerial functions	g) Pipe line fitter, sanitary engineer, anticorrosion inspector, gas reifier	107
	3. Low level of independence	h) Stove maker, PPU fitter, painter (plasterer), bricklayer	94
9 Functions of unskilled manual labor	2. Low level of independence	i) Auxiliary worker, loader, oiler, washer, navvy, auto-mechanic	245
		Total	3448

1.97

*Groups 3-7 have been omitted to save space.

auxiliary workers, riggers, oilers, washers, navvies, autome-
chanics — a total of 245 in all; the index of independence was
1.97 points).

Thus we found that in the same occupational group of workers, having roughly the same structure of technical functions,
there could be several kinds of positions constituting the creative framework of the job. At the same time, in studying the
level of on-the-job independence of workers by occupational
groups, we attempted to obtain a more precise idea of the demands made by foremen on workers. We found notable differences in these demands between the first and second subgroups.
To the question "What criteria do you use when you rate workers in some occupation?" we obtained the following ranked
series: from foremen in the first group — skill, discipline,
desire to work; from foremen in the second group — discipline,
experience, and skill. In the second case foremen's requirements were stricter; a behavioral feature (discipline) topped
the list, in contrast to foremen from the first group (here it
was skills, i.e., a productive and technical characteristic).[14]

To test our hypothesis we made a comparative analysis of
occupational groups in terms of two scales: "functional content of work" and "level of on-the-job independence" (see Table 3).

Three types of relationships between the positions of occupational groups on the two scales were clearly distinguishable in
the production organization of the enterprise: (1) a high degree of content of work functions and a low level of on-the-job
independence ($\Phi_\tau > \Phi_o$); (2) a low work content and relatively
high level of on-the-job independence ($\Phi_\tau < \Phi_o$); and (3) a
relative correspondence between the positions of the groups
on these scales ($\Phi_\tau = \Phi_o$).

An analysis of these kinds of relationships between Φ_τ and
Φ_o yields the following conclusions;

1. A high work content and relatively low level of on-the-job
independence were characteristic for occupational groups at
some borderline stage in the development of production,
namely, at the transition to comprehensive mechanization and

Table 3

Position of group on scale of "functional content of work" (Φ_T)	Position of group on scale of "on-the-job independence" (Φ_0)	Rating of position of group on both scales (Φ_T and Φ_0)	Position of group on scale of "functional content of work" (Φ_T)	Position of group on scale of "on-the-job independence" (Φ_0)	Rating of position of group on both scales (Φ_T and Φ_0)
I	IV	$\Phi_T > \Phi_0$	VI	IV	$\Phi_T < \Phi_0$
II	II	$\Phi_T = \Phi_0$	VII	I	$\Phi_T < \Phi_0$
III	VII	$\Phi_T > \Phi_0$	VIII	III	$\Phi_T < \Phi_0$
IV	VIII	$\Phi_T = \Phi_0$	IX	IX	$\Phi_T = \Phi_0$
V	V	$\Phi_T > \Phi_0$			

automation of the technological process (groups I, III, IV).

2. A low work content and relatively high level of on-the-job independence were characteristic of occupational groups in production activity at the threshold of comprehensive mechanization of technological processes (groups IV, VII, VIII) — so-called subsidiary and service production.

3. Identical positions on the scales were characteristic for occupational groups in stabilized kinds of production — mechanized, craft, and manufacturing (groups II, V, IX).

These relationships explain to some extent the insignificant Kendall coefficient of rank correlation that we obtained earlier (0.08). It is true that the positive sign of this coefficient indicates that there is a direct (although weak) relationship at enterprises between changing trends in the technological base and an increase in the on-the-job independence of workers. This reflects a certain pattern in the development of production revealed by empirical research into the specific conditions prevailing in the petroleum-extracting industry.

An important stage in our study was the testing of the consequences of the third hypothesis. If the functional content of work is weakly related to on-the-job independence, the following questions arise: what influence does the latter have on work attitudes, and how are both of these factors related to indices of the process of labor and the results of labor? To answer these questions required some rather laborious work to derive average indices (i) of work attitudes with respect to the process of labor and the results of labor for each occupation. We then derived average indices of work attitudes for the different occupational groups distinguished according to work content and degrees of on-the-job independence of the worker (see Tables 4 and 5).

Table 4

Ranked occupational groups according to work content	Attitude toward process of labor		Attitude toward results of labor	
	indices	ranks	indices	ranks
I	0.78	3	0.65	4
II	0.65	4	0.68	1
III	0.92	2	0.66	3
IV	0.57	5	0.56	6
V	0.49	6	0.41	7
VI	1.54	1	0.67	2
VII	0.37	8	0.61	5
VIII	0.39	7	0.38	8
IX	0.19	9	0.22	9

A calculation of Spearman's coefficients of correlation showed that the influence of the factor "on-the-job independence" on indices of work attitudes was quite significant and comparable with the influence of the factor "functional content of work" (see Table 6).

Table 5

Ranked occupa- tional groups according to on-the-job independence	Attitude toward process of labor		Attitude toward results of labor	
	indices — i*	ranks	indices — i*	ranks
I	0.24	1	0.28	1
II	0.70	6	0.55	3
III	0.44	2	0.33	2
IV	0.65	4	0.66	6
V	0.66	5	0.56	4
VI	0.54	3	0.58	5
VII	0.78	7	0.68	7

*Here we used the mean negative indices (−i). The lower the value of the index, the higher the index of work attitudes.

Table 6

Work attitude index	Functional content of work factor	On-the-job inde- pendence factor
For process of labor	0.70	0.54
For results of labor	0.57	0.84

In addition, our assumption that there were differences in the influence of these two factors on indices of the process of labor and the results of labor was confirmed. We see that the functional content of work is most closely related to indices for the process of labor ($\rho = 0.7$), while on-the-job independence is most closely related to the results of labor ($\rho = 0.84$). Indeed, the labor process depends to a considerable extent on technical and energy characteristics, equipment, the level of mechanization of labor, the materials used, the organization of the work place, etc., while the results of labor depend, in addition, on the goals of the work and on the workers' participation in defining the job task and in the planning and organization of his work. In certain production situations these factors may contradict one another. Indeed, to some extent this determines the contradictory nature of labor activity itself and the complexity of the process of shaping work attitudes.

The limited nature of our study with respect to its object and the scientific tools used preclude our making any broad generalizations on the basis of the empirical findings. Nonetheless, a number of concluding remarks with regard to the formulation of the problem are possible on the basis of our study.

There is no question that the further development of our conceptual framework in the direction proposed here will broaden our area of research into the problems of work attitudes and at the same time enable us to refine it more concretely. This will certainly be of use at both the theoretical and applied levels. The facts, on the basis of which generalizations and conclusions concerning work attitudes are formulated, stand in need of additional methodological clarification. It would seem that the conventional division of indices of work attitudes into "objective" and "subjective" has its limitations. The dialectic between the objective and subjective in the shaping of work attitudes can be understood most thoroughly only by delineating the characteristics of labor activity and its structure. In this connection it is not so much the relation between consciousness and behavior (as reflected in the division between subjective and objective indices) that is important as the blending of the elements of subjectivity and objectivity in labor activity: a worker acts simultaneously as both the subject of activity and as an object of management by the production organization of which he is a part. The indices of labor activity must somehow reflect this contradiction in the worker's position so that they may be brought more into line with the actual process of development of work attitudes. Our division into indices pertaining to the process of labor and the results of labor fulfills

this requirement only in the most general way. More studies
are needed in this direction.

There is also a need to refine our notions about specific factors. The division of factors into general (or resultant) and
specific is not a natural division that exists in itself; it has
meaning only within a certain frame of reference defined by
the subject matter of the inquiry. Thus, against a background
of global trends in the scientific-technical revolution, an improvement in work content and a broadening of the creative potential of a job constitute a universal resultant factor in the
development of work attitudes. The specific role of this factor
consists in the way it is purposefully and deliberately used in
a particular set of social and economic conditions: capitalism
confines work to production goals and is limited by a one-sided
development of the individual as a source of labor power; socialism makes use of the possibilities of work content to create the social conditions for the comprehensive development
of the individual, transforming him from a means into the end
of the development of production. The situation is similar with
the factor of on-the-job independence, which contains both a
universal and a specific component.

In moving on to an examination of the problem of work attitudes within a given social and economic system (in the particular case, socialism), the way in which the leading factors
of this process are utilized becomes universal. The specific
element is the particular combination of these factors inherent
in one or another production organization at a definite stage in
the development of its material and technological base, organizational structure, and the maturity of its social relations.
In other words, the specificity of factors is determined not by
their proximity to the work place but by their unique combination in the system of labor management in force at a particular
industrial enterprise (or association). The concept "social
production situation" might be useful here in the sense that it
is intended to encompass the interaction of organizational-
technical and social-organizational conditions through which
the universal factors are refracted. We can assume that the

empirically established variety of findings regarding work attitudes is related to the number of combinations of objective
and subjective factors in work activity. It is no accident that
studies of work attitudes among workers in Leningrad, Perm,
Ufa, Odessa, Al'met'evsk, and other cities, conducted on the
basis of roughly the same conceptual framework, have yielded
different statistical rankings of specific factors. In our opinion
this is an implicit reflection of the influence of the social production situation, which unfortunately, however, has not been
explicitly treated as a significant research problem.

The definition of on-the-job independence as a discrete object of inquiry is of both current and long-term significance.
In historical perspective one cannot regard the process of enriching work and broadening its creative potential as merely
the direct result of scientific-technical progress. One of the
major advantages of socialism is the planned improvement of
social relations, particularly management relations, which to
a large extent determine the creative potential of work provided
by its functional content, and which also play an important independent role in enriching work and in achieving a high level
of work performance.

In focusing attention on this interaction between the factors
of "the functional content of work" and "on-the-job independence" and their different effects on indices pertaining to the
process of labor and the results of labor, we can assume that
a certain mechanism is revealed here that shapes work attitudes under conditions of a concrete production activity in
which a definite relationship between these factors predomi-
nates. The latter is also important from the standpoint of the
unity of the methodological approach, since the proclamation
of the unity between material and social conditions of labor is
often confined to the theoretical portion of a study, while in the
empirical portion, one of these sets of conditions is ignored,
resulting in gross epistemological errors.

Finally, we feel that there is considerable practical potential
in the utilization of the results of studies of on-the-job independence of workers to improve the social and economic effec-

tiveness of labor. In the enterprise we studied, approximately
two thirds of the workers had only average or low opportunities
for demonstrating on-the-job independence, while the content
and regimen of their jobs constantly depended on the day-to-
day assignment of the volume of work. This means that the
effectiveness of work depends to a considerable extent on the
organizational capacities of administrative and managerial personnel. Under such conditions not only are workers very limited in their opportunities for taking part in planning and independent organization of their work and in its further improvement, but herein lies one of the reasons for the tremendous
volume of work that falls on the administrative and managerial
apparatus (accounting, coordination, filling out of documents,
etc.). As a result, inefficiencies in the organization of labor
at the enterprise increase, labor at the work place loses meaning, rationality and attractiveness are diminished.

Notes

1. See Chelovek i ego rabota, Moscow, 1967; G. N. Cherkasov, Sotsiologiia truda i profsoiuzy, Moscow, 1970; V. G. Pod-
markov, Vvedenie v promyshlennuiu sotsiologiiu, Moscow,
1973; Sotsiologiia i organizatsiia truda, Leningrad, 1973, etc.
2. See G. V. Badeeva, Sotsial'nye problemy truda v kom-
munisticheskom stroitel'stve, Moscow, 1971; I. I. Changli,
Trud, Moscow, 1973, etc.
3. See G. P. Koslova, "Izmenenie soderzhaniia truda v
sviazi s tekhnicheskim progressom," in Sotsial'nye problemy
truda i proizvodstva, Warsaw, 1969, p. 304.
4. K. Marx and F. Engels, Soch., vol. 23, p. 392.
5. The problems with which the investigator must deal in
taking this approach have been well described for the general
case in the article by V. A. Iadov and A. A. Kissel', "Udovle-
tvorennost' rabotoi: analiz empiricheskikh obobshchenii i
popytka ikh teoreticheskogo istolkovaniia," Sotsiologicheskie
issledovaniia, 1974, no. 1. p. 78.

6. Marx and Engels, Soch., vol. 23, p. 191.

7. The major part of the study was carried out in 1969-70 by associates of the Laboratory of Industrial Sociology of the "Tatneft'" Association, L. M. Adler, R. T. Akhmadeeva, E. V. Bobrovitskii, G. I. Valishvili, L. K. Golovach, A. D. Zav'ialova, M. D. Ivanchenko, A. M. Rudakov, and L. A. Frolova, under the direction of the author. The director of the petroleum-extracting board, R. T. Bulgakov, the secretary of the party committee, N. Z. Zakirova, and shop and section superintendents, foremen, and leading workers of the enterprise provided considerable help in carrying out the investigation.

8. We used a methodological approach proposed by Z. I. Fainburg, G. P. Kozlova, A. G. Zdravomyslov, and V. A. Iadov (see, for example, Chelovek i ego rabota, Moscow, 1967); the grouping of occupations in accordance with the functional content of work as presented below was prepared jointly with E. D. Tikhonova.

9. The questions: (a) How is a work task defined? (independently; a permanent task is assigned; a task extends over several days; tasks are assigned for a day; tasks are assigned several times per day); (b) How is the performance of a task usually organized? (completely independently; worker sometimes participates in its organization; does not participate in its organization; only carries it out); (c) To what degree is the performance of a task checked and monitored from without? (self-monitoring; monitoring from case to case; constant monitoring); (d) How is the accounting of work carried out? (self-accounting; documented accounting by the worker himself; visual accounting from without; documented accounting from without; accounting using technical means).

10. The complete list included indices for discipline, conscientiousness, observance of safety rules, technical creativity, initiative in achieving the results of labor, mutual help in the work process. It was compiled in the course of work with experts for the purpose of testing the first hypothesis and making our data comparable with the material used in the study Chelovek i ego rabota. With some modifications the indices

were tested by V. G. Tukumtsev at the Volga Togliatti Automobile Plant, showing that our measures are applicable beyond
the petroleum-extracting industry.

11. The procedure for calculating indices of work attitudes
was worked out by T. S. Kadibur. The indices were calculated
under his direction by S. K. and K. K. Shaidulin, students at
the N. A. Voznesenskii Institute of Finance and Economics,
Leningrad.

12. M. A. Alesina prepared the material for calculations.
The application of the β-coefficient cluster methods to the
analysis of the intercorrelation matrix was proposed and carried out by Iu. A. Shchegolev.

13. All nine occupational groups enumerated above were
used in the study. Table 1 gives only the two first and two last
groups as examples.

14. We should point out that we found that the foremen generally, throughout the enterprise, made rather stiff demands.
Discipline was voted in the first place, skill and desire to work
in second place, responsibility in third place, and initiative
in fourth place.

Bibliography

Akademiia nauk Kazakhskoi SSR. Institut ekonomiki. Upravlenie sotsial'nym razvitiem proizvodstvennykh kollektivov.
Alma Ata, 1975.

Akademiia nauk Moldavskoi SSR. Sotsial'naia aktivnost' rabotnikov promyshlennogo predpriiatiia. Kishinev, 1973.

Akademiia nauk SSSR. Institut istorii SSSR. Sotsial'nyi oblik
kolkhoznoi molodezhi po materialam sotsiologicheskikh
obsledovanii 1938 i 1969 gg. Moscow, 1976.

_____. Institut sotsiologicheskikh issledovanii. Aktivnost'
lichnosti v sotsialisticheskom obshchestve. Moscow, 1976.

Akademiia obshchestvennykh nauk pri TsK KPSS. Problemy
sovershenstvovaniia upravleniia sotsialisticheskoi ekono-
mikoi. Moscow, 1976.

_____. Uchastie mass v upravlenii proizvodstvom. Mos-
cow, 1976.

Alekseev, N. I. "On the Participation of Working People in
the Management of Production." Voprosy filosofii, 2, 1972.

_____ and Riazhskikh, I. A. "The Highest Organ of the Collective," in V. G. Afanas'ev, ed. Nauchnoe upravlenie
obshchestvom, no. 6. Moscow, 1972.

Andreichenko, G. V. "The Conception of 'Participation' of
Workers in the Management of Production in French Bourgeois Sociology." Sotsiologicheskie issledovaniia, 3, 1976.

Birman, A. "The Most Gratifying Task." Novy mir, 12, 1969.

127

Blinov, N. M. "The Satisfaction of Human Needs: A Most Important Social Function of Labor under Socialism." Sotsiologicheskie issledovaniia, 2, 1978.

Bogdanova, T. P. Trud i sotsial'naia aktivnost' molodezhi. Minsk, 1972.

Cherkasov, G. N. "Social Effectiveness: Essence and Criteria." Sotsiologicheskie issledovaniia, 1, 1978.

Fomin, V. A., ed. Nekotorye voprosy nauchnogo kommunizma. Moscow, 1967.

Iadov, V. A. "Let Us Look Facts in the Face." Voprosy filosofii, 5, 1965.

_____. "Who Does Not Like Work and Why." Literaturnaia gazeta, May 16, 1973.

_____, ed. Molodezh' i trud. Moscow, 1970.

_____, ed. Sotsial'no-psikhologicheskii portret inzhenera. Moscow, 1977.

_____ and Alekseeva, V. G. "The Scientific-Technical Revolution and the Personality of the Worker," in Profsoiuzy i kommunisticheskoe vospitanie trudiashchikhsia. Moscow, 1975.

Ivanov, B. N. "On the Question of a System of Indicators of Social and Political Activity of the Masses." Sotsiologicheskie issledovaniia, 3, 1978.

Ivanov, Iu. K. and Patrushev, V. D. "The Influence of Conditions of Work on Work Satisfaction in Agriculture." Sotsiologicheskie issledovaniia, 3, 1976.

Kapeliush, Ia. "In Favor of an Experiment." Literaturnaia gazeta, August 31, 1977.

Kharchev, A. G. and Golod, S. I. Professional'naia rabota zhenshchin i sem'ia. Leningrad, 1971.

Kosenko, O. I. "The Collective Elects Its Leader." Ekonomika i organizatsiia promyshlennogo proizvodstva, 1, 1977.

Krevnevich, V. V. "Automation as a Condition of Increasing the Content of Labor and Work Satisfaction." Sotsiologicheskie issledovaniia, 1, 1977.

Levin, B. M. Sotsial'no-ekonomicheskie potrebnosti: zakonomernosti formirovaniia i razvitiia. Moscow, 1974.

Liashenko, L. P. "The Attitude of Youth toward Agricultural Labor," in T. I. Zaslavskaia and V. A. Kalmyk, eds. Sotsial'no-ekonomicheskoe razvitie sela i migratsiia naseleniia. Novosibirsk, 1972.

_____ and Zaslavskaia, T. I. "Studying the Factors Which Shape Attitudes toward Agricultural Labor," in T. I. Zaslavskaia, ed. Sotsial'nye problemy trudovykh resursov sela. Novosibirsk, 1968.

Miasnikov, A. "Modernization Plus the Social Factor." Sotsialisticheskii trud, 11, 1976.

Mizerov, S. D. "The Role of Public Opinion of the Working Class in Socialist Management," in Akademiia obshchestvennykh nauk pri TsK KPSS. Problemy nauchnogo kommunizma, no. 9. Moscow, 1975.

Mukhachev, V. I. "Participation of Working Youth in the Management of Production." Sotsiologicheskie issledovaniia, 1, 1978.

_____ and Borovik, V. S. Rabochii klass i upravlenie proizvodstvom. Moscow, 1975.

Naumova, N. F. "Work and the Mode of Life," in V. I. Dobrynina, comp. Sovetskii obraz zhizn': segodnia i zavtra. Moscow, 1976.

_____ and Sliusarianskii, M. A. "Satisfaction in Work and Some Characteristics of the Personality," in Akademiia nauk SSSR. Institut konkretnykh sotsial'nykh issledovaniia. Sotsial'nye issledovaniia, no. 3. Moscow, 1970.

Orlov, A. "Participation of Working People in Management of Production and Indices of Its Effectiveness." Sotsialisticheskii trud, 5, 1978.

Osipov, G. N. and Shchepanskii, Ia. Sotsial'nye problemy truda i proizvodstva. Moscow, 1969.

Ostapenko, I. P. Rabochii klass v upravlenii proizvodstvom. Moscow, 1976.

Patrushev, V. D. and Shabashev, V. A. "The Influence of Social and Economic Conditions of Work on Collaboration and Mutual Help in the Production Collective." Sotsiologicheskie issledovaniia, 4, 1975.

Perevedentsev, V. "For All and for Each." Nash sovremennik, 1, 1974.

Podorov, G. M. "Sociological Studies of Labor Discipline at Enterprises in the Gorky Region." Sotsiologicheskie issledovaniia, 4, 1976.

Popova, I. M. Stimulirovanie trudovoi deiatel'nosti kak sposob upravleniia. Kiev, 1976.

Ratitskii, A. I. "Sociopsychological Aspects of Wages and Potential Mobility." Sotsiologicheskie issledovaniia, 2, 1978.

Romanov, O. V. "The Influence of Workers' Information about Production on their Social, Political, and Labor Activity." Sotsiologicheskie issledovaniia, 4, 1976.

Rudich, F. M. O sochetanii gosudarstvennykh i obshchestvennykh nachal v upravlenii proizvodstvom. Kiev, 1968.

Smirnov, V. A. "Constructing a Typology of Workers by Combining Objective and Subjective Indicators of Their Work Activity." Sotsiologicheskie issledovaniia, 1, 1977.

_____. "The Problem of Developing a Conscious Attitude toward Work among Working Youth." Sotsiologicheskie issledovaniia, 4, 1978.

_____ and Boikov, V. E. "The Brigade Contract and Communist Upbringing of Youth." Sotsiologicheskie issledovaniia, 2, 1978.

Sokol'nikov, Iu. L. "Socialist Labor Discipline and the Means of Improving It." Sotsiologicheskie issledovaniia, 1, 1976.

Stoliarova, I. E. "Some Social Indicators of the Formation of a Collective." Sotsiologicheskie issledovaniia, 2, 1975.

Sviridov, N. A. "Special Features of the Adaptation of the Individual to Complex Production Circumstances." Sotsiologicheskie issledovaniia, 2, 1977.

Stul', Ia. E. and Tishchenko, I. O. "Sociopsychological Principles of Management," in V. G. Afanas'ev, ed. Nauchnoe upravlenie obshchestvom, no. 4. Moscow, 1970.

Timush, A. Sotsial'nye protsessy na sele. Kishenev, 1975.

Vel'sh, A. G. "Motivational Orientations of Engineers of an Industrial Enterprise." Sotsiologicheskie issledovaniia, 3, 1975.

Volkov, Iu. E. "The Development of the Feeling of Being Master
of the Enterprise among Soviet Workers," in M. T. Iovchuk
and L. N. Kogan, eds. Dukhovnyi mir sovetskogo rabochego.
Moscow, 1972.

_____. "Problems of Developing Democratic Principles in
the Management of Socialist Production," in V. G. Afanas'ev,
ed. Nauchnoe upravlenie obshchestvom, no. 4, Moscow, 1970.

_____. "Social Activity of Working People and Some Prob-
lems of Its Development under Conditions of Mature Socialism," in Akademiia obshchestvennykh nauk pri TsK KPSS.
Problemy nauchnogo kommunizma, no. 10. Moscow, 1976.

_____. "Socialism and Production Democracy." Voprosy
filosofii, 1, 1968.

_____. Tak rozhdaetsia kommunisticheskoe samoupravlenie.
Moscow, 1965.

_____ and Loshkarev, Iu. S. Trudovoe vospitanie molodezhi.
Moscow, 1976.

Zaslavskaia, T. I., ed. Migratsiia sel'skogo naseleniia. Moscow, 1970.

Zdravomyslov, A. G. and Iadov, V. A. "The Results of an Empirical Investigation into Attitudes toward Work." Voprosy
filosofii, 4, 1964.

_____ and Iadov, V. A., eds. Trud i i razvitie lichnosti.
Leningrad, 1965.

_____, Rozhin, V. P. and Iadov, V. A. Chelovek i ego rabota.
Moscow, 1967.

About the Editor

Murray Yanowitch is currently Professor of Economics at Hofstra University. Educated at Columbia University, he has published numerous articles on Soviet affairs and is the co-editor of the journals Problems of Economics and International Journal of Sociology. With Bertram Silverman he co-edited The Worker in "Postindustrial" Capitalism, and with Wesley A. Fisher, Social Stratification and Mobility in the USSR. He is the author of Social and Economic Inequality in the Soviet Union.

DATE DUE

F '80	p.5.21		
S '82	PS21		
S '83	PS21		
F '83	PS 21		
OCT 2 3 1986			